D1204658

LINKING AUDITING AND METAEVALUATION

Applied Social Research Methods Series
Volume 11

Applied Social Research Methods Series

Series Editor:
LEONARD BICKMAN, Peabody College, Vanderbilt University
Series Associate Editor:
DEBRA ROG, National Institute of Mental Health

This series is designed to provide students and practicing professionals in the social sciences with relatively inexpensive softcover textbooks describing the major methods used in applied social research. Each text introduces the reader to the state of the art of that particular method and follows step-by-step procedures in its explanation. Each author describes the theory underlying the method to help the student understand the reasons for undertaking certain tasks. Current research is used to support the author's approach. Examples of utilization in a variety of applied fields, as well as sample exercises, are included in the books to aid in classroom use.

Volumes in this series:

LINKING AUDITING AND METAEVALUATION

Enhancing Quality in Applied Research

Thomas A. Schwandt
Edward S. Halpern

Applied Social Research Methods Series
Volume 11

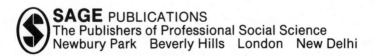

SAGE PUBLICATIONS
The Publishers of Professional Social Science
Newbury Park   Beverly Hills   London   New Delhi

Copyright © 1988 by Sage Publications, Inc.

For information address:

SAGE Publications, Inc.
2111 West Hillcrest Drive
Newbury Park, California 91320

SAGE Publications Inc.   SAGE Publications Ltd.
275 South Beverly Drive   28 Banner Street
Beverly Hills   London EC1Y 8QE
California 90212   England

SAGE PUBLICATIONS India Pvt. Ltd.
M-32 Market
Greater Kailash I
New Delhi 110 048 India

Printed in the United States of America

Library of Congress Cataloging-in-Publication Data

Schwandt, Thomas A.
    Linking auditing and metaevaluation.

    (Applied social research methods series ; v. 11)
    Bibliography: p.
    Includes index.
    1. Social sciences—Research—Evaluation.
I. Halpern, Edward Scott, 1952-   . II. Title.
III. Series.
H62.S36 1988   300'.72   87-12507
ISBN 0-8039-2967-6
ISBN 0-8039-2968-4 (pbk.)

FIRST PRINTING 1988

CONTENTS

FOREWORD

This book represents a major step forward in the development of tools and techniques by which the goodness of an inquiry can be procedurally assured and retrospectively assessed. It is especially useful in connection with inquiries guided by nonconventional paradigms, such as the naturalistic, the constructivist, the interpretive, the hermeneutic, the ethnographic, the qualitative, and others that have caught the imaginations of many of today's researchers, evaluators, and policy analysts. Nontraditional studies are found not only in education, but also in such diverse fields as psychology, sociology, political science, communication theory, nursing, occupational therapy, recreation, management, organizational theory, social work, and women's studies.

A pervasive and relatively intractable problem besetting such inquiries is that of establishing their merit. "Why," a consumer might ask, "should I believe this study's results? How can I tell whether the study meets criteria of goodness? What are appropriate criteria of goodness anyway?" The problem is compounded by the fact that any proposed criteria are *themselves* linked to some *particular* paradigm, so that studies carried out within *that* paradigm will inevitably appear to be more meritorious than will studies carried out in some other paradigm.

Tom Schwandt and Ed Halpern here propose an approach that permits the assessment of quality while remaining open to a variety of standards, depending on the paradigm guiding the study being assessed. This approach is based on the metaphor of *fiscal auditing*. In general, when a company, General Electric, say, hires an accounting firm such as Price, Waterhouse to audit its books, the auditor expects to deal with two issues: (1) Is the *accounting practice* used by the audited firm (read, *inquiry methodology* used by the audited investigator) within the purview of good professional practice? and (2) Is the *bottom line* (read, *findings*) "right"? Clearly, what is meant by "good professional practice" and "right" will depend on the particular paradigm at issue, but the two generic questions can be quite well addressed *regardless* of the paradigm used. In this book Schwandt and Halpern tell us how to do that. Their purpose is to unpack the auditing metaphor in ways that will help inquirers to assure the integrity and quality of their inquiries. The model they devise provides a framework for conceptualizing and formalizing the activity of peer criticism.

The publication of this volume is aptly timed. The emergence of new paradigms has raised serious questions about how merit can be established. Taken-for-granted approaches become problematic; indeed, concepts such as internal and external validity, reliability, and objectivity, mainstay criteria of traditional inquiry, appear quite inappropriate when ontological assumptions shift from realist to relativist, when epistemological assumptions shift from dualist, objective to monist, subjective, and when methodological assumptions shift from interventionist and controlling to hermeneutic. The auditing metaphor allows the inquirer to escape from the straitjacket of traditionalist standards while still holding him or her accountable for integrity and quality. The press for professionalism that surrounds all inquiry modes, but particularly evaluation and policy analysis, is likewise well served by this more formal mode of assessment. The emergence of standards, particularly those issued by the Joint Committee on Standards for Evaluation of Educational Programs, Projects, and Materials (and the soon-to-be-released Standards for Evaluations of Educational Personnel) is another indicator of the national concern for quality.

The auditing model proposed by Schwandt and Halpern has a number of advantages as a means of quality assurance. First, it has a wide range of applicability. Its major focus is on what might be called *retrovaluation,* that is, retrospective evaluation of an inquiry once it has been carried out. But the model may also be used in the development of the study plan or design (or comparable concept within nontraditional paradigms)—what might be called *provaluation,* as for example, in determining what ought to be placed in an audit trail, and what might be done to increase the probability that, at the end, quality criteria will be found to be satisfied. Finally, the model can be used during a study for quality *monitoring* purposes, as a basis for reflecting on progress to date and the extent to which provaluative considerations have been adequately managed.

Second, because of its independence from specific criteria or standards, the auditing model can be used not only in nontraditional studies but in any studies. There is no reason, for example, why even a closely controlled study, such as an experiment, cannot be audited.

Indeed, to do so would provide a check on an investigator's claims that conventional criteria, for example, reliability, have been met. Unfortunate instances of fabricated or altered data would certainly be less frequent than is currently the case should the practice of auditing become common.

Third, the audit can be effectively used regardless of the nature of the inquiry, whether research, evaluation, or policy analysis. These three forms of inquiry are distinctly different, despite common confusion of them as in the phrase, *evaluation research*. Nevertheless, they share a common methodology, particularly in nontraditional paradigms. Although the methodology may be employed toward different ends, methodological standards (those appropriate to the paradigm that is employed in each case) apply with equal weight. There cannot be a methodology in any paradigm that would be found to meet goodness criteria with respect to, say, research, but not with respect to evaluation or policy analysis.

Finally, the model justifies the labor required to implement it, including the apparently daunting task of compiling an audit trail. It is without a peer as a means for organizing data, making them quickly accessible to retrieval. Further, data are not only conveniently catalogued but they are also cross-referenced and related by the audit trail. The logical framework that emerges significantly assists the tasks of theorizing (grounded theory), of sensing relationships (including a developing sense of what might be missing), and of writing. These are important payoffs indeed. The audit forces a kind of self-discipline that would be hard to achieve in other ways.

The book itself is an exemplar of good writing. It is, first of all, extremely readable and understandable. Some presumptions are made about the reader's background, of course. The reader is expected to be *au courant* with current models and procedures of evaluation, to be familiar with the concept of nontraditional paradigms and how these paradigms differ from the conventional paradigm, and to be knowledgeable about both traditional and emergent methodologies. That is to say, the authors address themselves to informed and sophisticated practitioners of the art of inquiry. Nevertheless they avoid arcane language and convoluted writing to a remarkable degree.

Second, the book is extraordinarily well organized, perhaps reflecting the instructional systems technology background of one of the writers. The material is presented in a logical, spiraling format that facilitates learning while leading the reader ever forward. Techniques of retrospection of earlier chapters, redundancy to reinforce and emphasize important concepts, and foreshadowing material yet to come are freely and well used. Questions likely to arise in readers' minds are anticipated and dealt with at the most appropriate points.

Finally, the book abounds with helpful, practical features. Each chapter is followed by exercises that challenge readers' understanding and test their ability to use basic concepts, most often in the readers' own situations. Later chapters present and examine applications. Charts and tables in the body of the text provide detailed guidance. Well-chosen references lead readers to sources that can clarify and extend the content of the book.

Of course there are a number of caveats of which readers should remain mindful. First, auditing is but *one* mode whereby an inquiry can be evaluated (or, in the case of evaluation, metaevaluated, to follow the authors' usage). It has been well-accepted practice that an inquirer should himself or herself provide the evidence needed to establish the quality of the published inquiry, for example, evidence attesting to the validity and reliability of instrumentation. This practice has not served the profession badly, although it is open to serious abuse that is sometimes very hard to detect. The development of various standards, such as the *Standards for Educational and Psychological Tests;* the *Standards for Evaluations of Educational Programs, Projects, and Materials,* or the *Standards for Evaluation Programs,* provides another approach, although as I have suggested, and Schwandt and Halpern document, these standards are intimately tied to a particular paradigm of application. The refereeing process that characterizes mainstream professional journals is another means, as is the opportunity often afforded to critique or make rejoinders to particular published reports. And it is certainly the case that the audit process cannot by itself deal with all questions of rigor, trustworthiness, and authenticity that might be raised. Selective, purposeful application is the key.

Second, as Schwandt and Halpern point out, the function of an audit is "to attest to or verify quality, not to create it." All the auditing in the world cannot compensate for an inquiry that is sloppily planned and implemented. It is the case that if an inquirer carefully incorporates audit procedures from the inception of an inquiry, it is unlikely that quality will be found wanting. Nevertheless, an auditor can no more ameliorate or eliminate inherent problems than can a statistician breathe life into inappropriate or badly collected data.

Third, the auditor should not take the metaphor too literally. Fiscal auditing, the metaphoric root, evolved within a conception of organizational behavior that emphasizes tight coupling, rational decision making, rule-following, and the like. We must be careful lest the auditing process provide a reason for demanding more structure than is healthy, particularly at a time when new paradigms are emerging and traditional conceptions of, for example, the nature of evaluation, or the differences between research, evaluation, and policy analysis, are being reexamined. These emergent ideas need elbow room. Every effort must be made to prevent the emergence of a form of auditing that is value-dissonant with emergent ideas about inquiry itself. Our concern with accountability ought not to be permitted to override our creativity, our search for more informed and sophisticated constructions to guide our inquiries.

Fourth, we must take care to resist hasty efforts to reach an accommodation on standards. The world of inquiry, presently in intellectual ferment, might well appear to profit from reaching some conventional agreements about what constitute adequate standards of excellence, but it is unlikely that such an accommodation is reachable in the near future. Indeed, it is unlikely that an accommodation can come about in any way except through protracted dialectic interchanges among holders of different views. No existing paradigm is likely to engulf the others because of the inherent superiority of its construction, or because the others can be shown to be nothing more than special cases of the first, or because the several paradigms will be found to be complementary in some way (the discovery-verification or qualitative-quantitative distinctions notwithstanding). At this point we must content ourselves with having found a *process* that will be workable with any set of standards that are conceptually acceptable to the adherents of that paradigm to which those standards putatively apply.

Finally, we must take care not to create a new orthodoxy with the audit process, particularly in ways that would reinforce conventional inquiry modes at the expense of the emergent. Conventional ways of assessing the integrity and quality of an inquiry have an absolutist quality that undoubtedly arises as a consequence of the realist ontology on which the prevailing paradigm is based. When there is believed to be an objective reality operating according to immutable natural laws, an inquiry can be sound—by definition—if, and only if, it captures that reality or a reasonable approximation of it. Emergent modes of inquiry tend to operate from a relativist ontology; that does not mean that "anything goes" but it does require that all informed and sophisticated constructions be given a fair hearing. Until we are able to reach an accommodation on standards, relativism seems the safer course; we cannot afford to take the "true believer" stance.

This book makes no pretense at solving all these problems, or, for that matter, even addressing them in any systematic way. What it *does* is to provide a detailed elaboration of a metaphor that has great promise for dealing with issues surrounding the integrity and quality of an inquiry. As such it represents a significant and far-reaching contribution. It also illustrates the abiding commitment of nontraditional inquirers to take goodness questions seriously, at least as seriously as their conventional colleagues. In my judgment the proposals of Schwandt and Halpern deserve careful attention and systematic trial.

The authors will benefit enormously from feedback provided by those colleagues who may try these ideas in one form or another. I invite the readers of this book to think about possible applications in their own interest areas and to carry them out. Information about such experiences will enable the revision, refinement, improvement, and extension of these materials. It has been said that the best theories are the shortest-lived; they are so heuristic that they quickly give rise to insights and data that make their rapid replacement possible. It is my hope that this book will prove to fall into that class.

—Egon G. Guba
Bloomington, Indiana

PREFACE

For more than a century, public accountants have been called upon to perform investigative audit work and subsequently to deliver informed, independent, professional opinions on management's activities. In its early history in the United States, the auditing function occasionally assumed some unique forms. For example, in 1923 the accounting firm of Haskins & Sells issued the following statement of certification (cited in Previts, 1985, p. 53):

Statement by
Haskins & Sells
Certified Public Accountants

Pursuant to engagement, we have reviewed the manuscript of your book *Analysis of the Interchurch Report on the Steel Strike* for the purpose of verifying, by comparison with their stated sources, the citations, quotations, statistics, and figures contained therein; and

WE HEREBY CERTIFY:
That all citations are accurate;
That all quotations, including excerpts in which the sequence of original passages has for clearness or brevity been varied, are accurate as to text and, in our opinion, fairly represent the meaning of their original context;
That all statistics and figures quoted have been verified by comparison with the documents from which quoted and those subject to mathematical proof have been so proved; and
That all statistics are presented and used in accordance with generally accepted statistical practices.

(Signed) HASKINS & SELLS.

Though no longer typical of the kind of work performed by financial auditors, this statement clearly conveys the auditor's objectives of examining, verifying, and attesting to the quality of some product or procedure. Since the passage of the Securities Acts in the United States in 1933-1934, which provided the impetus for the development of financial auditing as a primary function of the certified public accountant (CPA), the accounting profession has embarked upon a variety of efforts to enhance its ability to examine and attest to the use of sound financial accounting and reporting practices.

The auditor's concern with quality—how to define it, how to achieve it, how to verify it—forms the backdrop for this book. We believe it is instructive to examine in greater detail how auditors address these issues in quality and to explore the transfer of auditing concepts and strategies to the professional practice of sociobehavioral inquiry. Our general focus is that subset of inquiry (e.g., evaluation, policy analysis, applied social science) conducted expressly as a professional service to inform policy or decision making. Our general interest is in systematic approaches and techniques for monitoring, enhancing, and attesting to the quality of that service.

This book is one outcropping of this broad-based investigation. In it, we focus on evaluation in general and naturalistic evaluation in particular, and we examine how notions from financial auditing can be applied to the practice of establishing and attesting to the quality of evaluations.

We have chosen to focus on the interrelationships of evaluation, metaevaluation, and auditing in this book for several reasons. First, evaluation is clearly a professional service, and both providers (evaluators) and consumers of that service are naturally concerned with its quality. Second, metaevaluation (the practice of evaluating evaluations) is recognized as a legitimate approach for verifying the quality of evaluations. It might be said that metaevaluation is to evaluation as auditing is to accounting. Third, we think it advisable to investigate a systematic approach to metaevaluation that is resonant with the needs and concerns of both providers and consumers of evaluation. In our opinion, auditing is one such approach. Auditing helps formalize the activity of peer criticism of evaluation and provides consumers of evaluation with a somewhat familiar frame of reference for understanding what metaevaluation is intended to achieve. Finally, we have chosen to illustrate the application of auditing to evaluating qualitative or naturalistic evaluations because both evaluators and consumers of evaluation have been seeking assurances of its technical quality and integrity.

This book is intended primarily for evaluation practitioners as well as teachers, advanced undergraduate and graduate students. Practicing evaluators and evaluators-in-training will find the information presented here useful for enhancing the quality of their procedures, and ultimately, their products. Evaluators facing the task of conducting a metaevaluation will find a comprehensive methodology for checking the quality of an evaluation. Consumers and sponsors of evaluation will find the explication of an audit framework found in Chapters 1, 2, and 3 useful in understanding what metaevaluation is designed to achieve.

Several caveats should be kept in mind when reading this book: First, what is presented as an auditing model and strategy is an ideal type that requires adaptations and modifications in view of each user's unique set of circumstances. Second, this is a work of translation. Whenever one attempts to translate a model, set of concepts, or group of associated practices from one field to another there is always the danger of forcing a fit or of overextending the analogy. In our enthusiasm for presenting this approach, we do not mean to imply a one-to-one correspondence between the practices of auditing and metaevaluation. Third, this is an introduction to the links between auditing and metaevaluation. Many issues regarding the development of standards, self-regulatory practices, requirements for admission to the profession, legal and ethical matters, and so forth are not discussed here.

Multiple influences led to this undertaking. One of us began exploring auditing as a technique for both improving and attesting to the quality of naturalistic inquiries while he was a graduate student at Indiana University. His dissertation (Halpern, 1983) laid much of the groundwork for the present book. The other began researching the links between auditing and evaluation while employed as an evaluation specialist with the professional education division of a major international auditing and consulting firm. This book really had its genesis there, in an environment where auditing was not only a professional client service but part of the very culture of the organization itself.

Informal conversations between us gradually led to more formal collaboration. In October, 1984 we delivered a presession on auditing qualitative evaluations at the joint meeting of the Evaluation Network and the Evaluation Research Society (now, the American Evaluation Association). The interest in and response to our presession, as well as to other sessions on auditing presented at the conference, further stimulated our thinking about the issue. We have also benefited from the experiences of our colleagues who have shared their thoughts and efforts, including Egon Guba, who first introduced the notion of auditing naturalistic inquiries, Jeri Nowakowski, Bob Covert and his graduate students at the University of Virginia, Jennifer Greene and her students at Cornell University, Oliver Cummings, and Hugh McRoberts and others from the Office of the Auditor General in Canada. All of these individuals as well as our editors and two anonymous reviewers had a hand in shaping our ideas, though we alone are responsible for what appears on the following pages.

Finally, we wish to thank Lynn Rendall, who helped track down many an auditing reference for us and Sarah Gooden and Maggie Wade, who assisted in typing the manuscript.

Tom Schwandt
Ed Halpern
Oak Park, Illinois

1

Linking Auditing and Metaevaluation

Audit is the process of the evaluation of something proposed or asserted.
—Schandl, 1978

As a professional service develops and matures, both the providers and consumers of that service naturally become concerned about its quality. Providers design and implement quality controls for their plans, procedures, and products in order to enhance the effectiveness and usefulness of their services. Consumers or clients seek assurances of the integrity and quality of the providers' services and products.

In the years since the field of evaluation has entered what Madaus and others (1983) have called its "Age of Professionalization," individuals who offer, sponsor, and use the professional service of evaluation have become increasingly concerned with the quality of evaluation plans, procedures, and findings. This concern is evident in efforts to design evaluations that are responsive to stakeholder needs, to incorporate into evaluation plans procedures that facilitate the use of findings, to verify the quality of evaluations through metaevaluations, and to set standards that serve as benchmarks for the professional practice of evaluation.

This book contributes to this dialogue by focusing on metaevaluation as one means of enhancing quality. From the perspective of evaluation stakeholders (e.g., sponsors, clients, consumers), metaevaluation (the practice of evaluating evaluations) is a means of providing some assurance of the quality of evaluation procedures and findings. From the point of view of providers or those who actually conduct evaluations, metaevaluation is a means of monitoring or enhancing quality control.

On the following pages, we introduce financial auditing as a model and strategy for metaevaluation. Both auditing and metaevaluation are disciplined forms of inquiry in which professional judgment is used to render an opinion about quality. Metaevaluation requires exercising professional judgment to determine whether an evaluation was performed properly and whether its findings and conclusions are trustworthy. Likewise, auditing requires judgment to determine whether management has properly prepared its financial statements and whether those statements fairly represent historical financial conditions. The auditing profession maintains and continually updates a conceptual and pragmatic framework or structure that both directs and informs the art and science of auditing. This book examines that structure in part and attempts to answer the question, "What can we learn from the principles and practices of auditing that might improve the conduct of metaevaluation, and, therefore, the quality of evaluation?"

This book has four objectives. The first is to introduce readers to critical auditing concepts and practices so that they might see how an auditing framework can help inform the organization and execution of metaevaluation. Chapters 1, 2, and 3 are primarily directed at this objective. Chapter 1 provides definitions of auditing and metaevaluation and compares the two practices in terms of professional roles, objectives, and salient characteristics. Chapter 2 discusses issues of standards, procedures, and accepted principles in the two fields, pointing out similarities and highlighting differences in formalization and maturity of the practices. Chapter 2 also displays a general model for auditing an evaluation. Chapter 3 examines the forms and functions of the auditor's report.

A second objective is to illustrate the application of an audit model to the task of verifying (evaluating) the quality of a qualitative or naturalistic evaluation. Chapters 4 and 5 are devoted to this objective. Chapter 4 provides background information for this particular illustration and then discusses in detail the task of constructing an audit trail from the point of view of the auditee (evaluator). Chapter 5 presents an audit work program—a set of procedures—that an auditor (metaevaluator) might follow in examining the quality of naturalistic evaluations.

A third objective is embedded in the extended example that comprises Chapters 4 and 5. We hope readers will see that the audit trail and audit work program can serve the needs of evaluators who are concerned about *improving* the quality of naturalistic evaluations as well as the needs of metaevaluators charged with the task of *attesting* to the quality of these evaluations. A prospective look at what an auditor will be seeking will help the evaluator to build quality into the evaluation. A detailed set of procedures for conducting an audit will help metaevaluators approach the task of checking quality in an organized and systematic fashion.

Finally, a fourth objective is concerned with demonstrating that an audit model has applications beyond the illustration we have chosen. Chapter 6 addresses this objective. It provides suggestions for constructing an audit trail and audit work program to meet the needs of other inquiry situations, other inquiry methodologies, and other inquiry paradigms.

DEFINITIONS AND APPLICATIONS OF AUDITING

Auditing is generally regarded as a process of evaluation resulting in a judgment. The American Accounting Association (1973) provides the following general definition of auditing:

> A systematic process of objectively obtaining and evaluating evidence regarding assertions about economic actions and events to ascertain the degree of correspondence between these assertions and established criteria and communicating the results to interested users. (p. 2)

This definition reveals that auditing is a type of disciplined inquiry:

- "a systematic process"—an auditor's review and examination is planned, orderly, and methodical;
- "objectively obtaining and evaluating evidence"—an audit is an independent, empirical investigation;
- "ascertain the degree of correspondence between assertions and established criteria"—auditing involves the exercise of professional judgment in applying a set of criteria;
- "communicating the results to interested users"—the outcome of an audit examination is made public.

The strategy of auditing some procedure, operation, outcome, or product against a set of standards or criteria has been used in a variety of ways. For example, in medicine, an audit methodology developed for the Joint Commission on Accreditation of Hospitals (Jacobs, 1973) has been applied to a review of medical records (Ashbaugh & McKean, 1976; Clemenhagen et al., 1985). The evaluation involves a retrospective analysis of the quality of medical care by auditing information contained in medical records against a set of standards or criteria for medical procedures and outcomes. Criteria (based on expert consensus) include indications/justification for hospital admission, appropriateness of admission, and application of diagnostic and treatment protocols. Other common, and perhaps more familiar, applications of auditing include financial, operational, and performance audits.

Financial Attest Audit

Throughout this book, we will be using this type of audit as our model or analogue for metaevaluation. A financial audit is a retrospective "examination of a company's financial statements for the purpose of forming an opinion of their fairness in conformity with generally accepted accounting principles" (Taylor & Glezen, 1982, p. 4). This type of audit serves a quality assurance function for readers of financial statements because the auditor attests to the integrity and dependability of management's financial reporting. Schandl (1978) refers to this as an attest audit, the expression of an opinion—an attestation—concerning the fairness and dependability of a set of financial statements. This kind of audit performed by an independent certified public accountant (CPA) is also called a "financial compliance audit" (Meigs et al., 1982) because it is concerned with determining compliance with a set of standards (generally accepted accounting principles) for financial accounting and reporting.

Operational/Management Audit

These types of audits are analogous to formative evaluations (McClintock, 1986). Most often conducted by internal auditors, an operational or management audit may focus on any or all of the following aspects of an organization: efficiency, effectiveness, economy, or performance. Edds (1980) states that the overall objective of operational auditing is to assist all levels of management in the effective discharge of their responsibilities by furnishing them with objective analyses, appraisals, recommendations and pertinent comments concerning the activities reviewed. (p. 30)

These audits may include an examination of the use of organizational resources or a review of information systems, internal controls, policies, procedures, and organizational structure. In addition, they may be conducted only in specific departments or divisions like marketing, personnel, or production. Operational or management audits are not attest work, rather they are what Schandl (1978) calls "attention-directing audits" designed to call management's attention to some aspect of internal operations. These types of audits are often used by management as a means of quality control.

Performance/Program Audit

This is a special type of operational audit that combines aspects of the former with an examination of program results or effectiveness. Brown, Gallagher, and Williams (1982) define performance auditing as a

custom crafted analysis of specific aspects of program efficiency and effectiveness. It differs from financial auditing in that [it] deals with a combination of financial and nonfinancial measures and usually must define a unique set of measurements and standards for each audit that is undertaken. (p. 12)

Performance audits are most often used to examine the extent to which public programs were operated efficiently and effectively. Brown and his associates note that three types of information are collected in these examinations: (1) information about resources used in rendering a particular service, (2) information about the quality of the service rendered or the goods produced, and (3) information about program results. Rothwell (1984) emphasizes that a program audit looks at the achievement of program objectives in terms of compliance with stated goals.

The U.S. General Accounting Office (GAO) performs a type of program or performance audit in its examination of federal programs, functions, and activities. The GAO standards for auditing (Comptroller

General of the United States, 1981, p. 12) indicate that the scope of government auditing may include: (1) an examination of financial transactions, accounts, and reports to determine compliance with applicable laws and regulations, (2) a review of efficiency and economy in the use of resources, and (3) an examination of program results to determine if objectives are being met and desired results are being achieved.

Inquiry Audits

An audit strategy can also be used as a tool for peer review or quality control of research and evaluation studies. Consider the following examples: (1) given a typology of validity considerations (e.g., Cook & Campbell, 1979; Krathwohl, 1985), one might audit a particular quasi-experimental study against those considerations; (2) given a set of standards for what constitutes sound ethnographic design (e.g., Goetz & LeCompte, 1984), one might audit an ethnographic inquiry against those standards; (3) given Lincoln and Guba's (1985; Guba, 1981) criteria for assessing the trustworthiness of naturalistic inquiries, one might audit the procedures and findings of a naturalistic inquiry against those criteria; (4) given the Joint Committee's Standards (1981) for educational evaluation, one might audit a particular evaluation against those standards.

In sum, auditing is an evaluation tool for checking quality. It is a procedure for evaluating some process or outcome against an established set of criteria. As a means of providing quality assurance, auditing has applications in several disciplines including, medicine, accounting, and social science inquiry. As a tool for checking the quality of inquiry, it can be applied to a variety of types of studies (i.e., research, evaluation, policy studies), to a variety of inquiry methodologies (i.e., quasi-experimental designs, ethnographies) and in any inquiry paradigm (i.e., postpositivist, interpretive, naturalistic). In this book, we will explore one particular application, namely, linking auditing to the practice of evaluating naturalistic evaluations.

AUDITING AS A TOOL FOR METAEVALUATION

In the context of evaluation, an audit has been defined as "an independent examination and verification of the quality of an evaluation plan, the adequacy with which it was implemented, the accuracy of the results, and the validity of conclusions" (Joint Committee, 1981, p. 149). This places auditing squarely within the domain of metaevaluation. Both auditing and metaevaluation share several general characteristics: Both are types of evaluations involving systematic examinations, made by professionals who, exercise their judgment in collecting and weighing evidence, to determine adherence to some set of criteria, and who report their findings to interested parties.

Metaevaluation (Scriven, 1969; Stufflebeam, 1974, 1978; Cook & Gruder, 1978) is the practice of evaluating evaluations. It assumes that good evaluation requires some type of check on its technical quality, freedom from bias, usefulness, and so forth. Stufflebeam (1981) has defined metaevaluation as:

> The process of delineating, obtaining, and using descriptive and judgmental information about the utility, practicality, ethics, and technical adequacy of an evaluation in order to guide the evaluation and publicly to report on its strengths and weaknesses. (p. 151)

Cook and Gruder (1978) identify three research traditions informing the practice of metaevaluation: (1) secondary data analysis, (2) ratings of evaluations against a set of criteria (e.g., Bernstein & Freeman, 1975), and (3) "research on research." They also discuss four models for metaevaluation that takes place subsequent to an original evaluation: (1) an essay review of an evaluation report, (2) a review of the literature about a specific program, (3) an empirical reevaluation of an evaluation, and (4) an empirical reevaluation of multiple data sets about the same program. Other metaevaluation procedures include management systems for judging the quality of evaluations (e.g., Chelimsky, 1983) and audits of program effectiveness measurement (McRoberts & Soper, 1985). Generally, all of these approaches are employed for the same reason, namely, to assess the technical quality of one or more original evaluations. Just what constitutes quality is the subject of Chapter 2. We shall see that definitions of quality vary and that metaevaluation procedures vary accordingly.

How can financial attest auditing as a strategy for making an independent, third-party examination inform our understanding of the practice of metaevaluation? The remainder of this chapter attempts to answer this question by first looking at some salient characteristics that both types of examinations have in common.

REASONS FOR MAKING A THIRD-PARTY EXAMINATION

Independent, financial audits are conducted because consumers of financial reports seek assurances that the information supplied to them by the auditee is complete, accurate, and objective. Unaudited financial statements create the possibility of a "credibility gap" (Meigs et al., 1982). Users of financial statements want some assurance that management was not biased, careless, or deliberately deceitful in presenting the picture of its company's financial health. Hence, information users look to the auditor for an independent opinion regarding the fairness and dependability of management's reported financial position. To protect the public's interest, the Securities and Exchange Commission (SEC) requires an independent auditor's examination for all its registrants as a means of qualifying them for sale to the public.

Financial audits are not expected to take the place of policies, procedures, and practices (i.e., quality control mechanisms) that management should employ to ensure the integrity of its financial operations and the dependability of its financial reporting. Similarly, *an audit of an evaluation is not intended to replace methods (for example, triangulation, member checks, stakeholder participation) that an evaluator would use to enhance the quality of an evaluation.* The primary purpose of an audit of evaluation activities and reporting is to attest to or verify quality, not to create it. Improving or enhancing quality is a secondary benefit, or by-product of the auditing process.

It could be argued that consumers should make their own assessment of a company's reported financial position before deciding to invest, and most wise investors inevitably do just that. However, given the complexity of accounting and financial reporting practices, as well as the inability to access a company's proprietary, unpublished documentation, users of financial information are not always best equipped to make this assessment. As Edds (1980, p. 5) points out, information users require the assistance of an auditor for a variety of reasons:

(1) they have limited or no access to the auditee's documents and records needed to verify the auditee's claims;
(2) they lack the skill necessary to analyze and interpret the information;
(3) they lack access to corroborative information supporting the documents and records offered by the auditee; and/or
(4) they have insufficient resources to carry out the examination.

A metaevaluation is conducted for much the same reason that an audit is performed, namely, to provide users of the evaluation report with an outsider's opinion on the quality of the inquiry design, implementation, and analysis. Evaluation consumers, much like users of financial statements, seek assurances that evaluation procedures were appropriate and that findings were trustworthy and accurate. Furthermore, the reasons listed above that characterize the need of financial information users for an independent, financial audit also speak to the need of evaluation consumers for a third-party, metaevaluator's opinion.

In our experience, a second, less apparent reason for auditing evaluations is to prepare inquirers psychologically for an open, public scrutiny of their evaluations. We have learned that an inquirer facing the prospects of an audit is more likely to document procedures carefully and less likely to make decisions (in design, interpretation, or analysis) that are questionable. Empirical research is needed to determine whether the existence of an evaluation auditing function, or even the expectation of an audit, results in more careful and improved performance. However, a similar, secondary benefit is claimed for independent, financial auditing (Edds, 1980; Holmes & Burns, 1979).

The demand for financial auditing arises from information user's needs and governmental and legislative requirements. Clients (auditees) engage the services of auditors because they believe that auditors can help improve their operations and management activities, and because, in many cases, an auditor's examination is mandated.

The impetus for audits of evaluation activities is similar. Evaluators (clients) may request the services of an auditor to attest to the integrity and trustworthiness of their studies. This was the case in the audit of the Evaluation Research Center's evaluation of the 1983 joint conference of the Evaluation Research Society and the Evaluation Network (Covert & Stahlman, 1984) and the audit of the NIE project investigating the impact of educational service agencies on implementing P.L. 94-142 (Education for All Handicapped Children Act) in rural school districts (see Skrtic, 1985; Skrtic et al., 1985).

Audits of evaluation activities may also be initiated by federal agencies, as for example, the audits of program effectiveness measurement carried out by the Office of the Auditor General in Canada (Hudson & McRoberts, 1984) and the activity of the U.S. General Accounting Office (see Comptroller General of the United States, 1981).

Audits of evaluations are not nearly as commonplace as audits of financial statements. Considering the relative maturity of the professional practices of accounting and evaluation, this is not surprising. There has been substantial professional development in evaluation in recent years (Madaus, Stufflebeam, & Scriven, 1983), yet evaluation does not yet exhibit the characteristic set of traits that mark it as a special professional community (see, for example, Goode, 1957; Larson, 1977). This need not preclude a careful look at how evaluators can improve their craft both for their own benefit and for the benefit of their clients.

We believe that this examination of auditing is timely in view of recent efforts at self-monitoring (e.g., the development of evaluation standards). It anticipates a more organized approach to evaluating the quality of evaluation as a client service, and herein lies the advantage of considering auditing as a model for metaevaluation. Like other metaevaluation approaches, it promises to enhance the validity and credibility of evaluation procedures and findings. Yet, it differs from these approaches in that it offers a systematic framework or method-ology in which to conduct responsible criticism of evaluation. This framework is instructive for both evaluators and their clients. Evaluators can use this framework to organize and direct their metaevaluation activities and to help evaluation consumers more clearly understand the objectives of metaevaluation.

To be sure, the audit model for metaevaluation entails some added costs. Compiling an audit trail (see Chapter 4) will require additional time for those evaluators not accustomed to documenting their procedures carefully. We view this as a declining cost as evaluators learn to how to integrate documentation procedures into their day-to-day activities. The cost of the audit will most likely have to be added to the cost of the evaluation. Given a well-prepared audit trail, this cost is not prohibitive. Most audits can be completed in seven to ten days. Clients must perceive the added value of an audit to be willing to incur these costs. There are no simple solutions to this problem. To paraphrase Cook and Gruder (1978, p. 47), we believe that the future of auditing evaluations rests largely with clients who are interested in improving the quality of the evaluations they are funding and who are prepared to experiment with auditing as a means of improving quality.

PARTIES TO AN EXAMINATION

Table 1.1 displays the three major parties in both an audit and a metaevaluation: (1) the third-party examiner, (2) the client whose

TABLE 1.1
Parties to an Examination

Party	Financial Audit	Metaevaluation
Third-party examiner	auditor	metaevaluator
Client	auditee (corporation, government agency, partnership, etc.)	evaluator(s) conducting the original evaluation and authoring the evaluation report
Stakeholders	information users (stockholders; financial institutions, etc.)	consumers of the evaluation report (stakeholders; members of the policy-shaping community)

operations are being examined, and (3) those individuals with a stake in the outcome of the examination. The parties to an audit include the auditor, the auditee or client, and information users. The auditee may be an entire business corporation, an entire government department or agency, a nonprofit organization, or any operating unit of these entities (Edds, 1980). Information users are groups of people (stakeholders) with legitimate needs for information (usually financial) about the auditee. They may include directors, shareholders, potential investors, financial institutions, government regulatory agencies (for example, the Securities and Exchange Commission [SEC]), investment analysts, and so forth.

The parties to a metaevaluation include the metaevaluator, the evaluator(s) who conducted the evaluation and wrote the evaluation report (the client), and consumers of the evaluation (stakeholders). Consumers are likely to be members of the agency that commissioned the evaluation study, funders, program developers, persons affected by the intervention being evaluated, and other individuals comprising what Cronbach and others (1980) have identified as the "policy-shaping community." Just as an auditee would commission an audit and engage an auditor to perform a third-party examination, an evaluator would contract with a metaevaluator to review his or her study and to provide a third-party opinion about evaluation quality.

ROLE AND QUALIFICATIONS
OF THE THIRD-PARTY EXAMINER

Auditors and metaevaluators perform similar roles depending on their relationship to the client (auditee or evaluator) and the nature of the audit examination. Table 1.2 displays a parallel view of these roles. Stufflebeam (1974, 1981) has described two roles for the metaevaluator:

- The *formative role* of guiding evaluation—an examination conducted during an evaluation to aid evaluators in making decisions about planning, conducting, interpreting, and reporting, and
- The *summative role* of publicly attesting to the strengths and weaknesses of an evaluation—an examination performed at the conclusion of an evaluation to report on its overall merit.

In the formative role, a metaevaluator acts as a consultant to the evaluator and performs his or her work internally and simultaneous to the evaluation activity. In the summative role, a metaevaluator performs an attestation. This is a retrospective activity performed by an independent, external agent upon completion of the evaluation. The metaevaluator attests to the quality of the process and product of the evaluation by comparing it to some set of evaluation standards. Here, the metaevaluator reviews the conduct and product of the evaluation after the evaluation has been completed and gives an opinion on its quality.

In financial auditing, the roles of internal and external auditor are similar to the roles of formative and summative metaevaluator, respectively. Internal and external (or independent) auditors are distinguished on the basis of their organizational affiliation, or more precisely, on their relationship to the client (auditee). Internal auditors are employees of the organizations whose activities they audit. They are often referred to as the eyes and ears of management. Their activity has the overall aim of improving the operations of the auditee. The Institute of Internal Auditors (1978, p. 1) defines internal auditing as "an independent appraisal function established within an organization to examine and evaluate its activities as a service to the organization." Notice that internal auditors act independently in forming their professional opinions, yet their studies are used by management to enhance or improve its operations. Similarly, formative metaevaluators act independently, yet on behalf of the evaluator or evaluation team.

TABLE 1.2
Roles of the Third-Party Examiner

Purpose	Financial Auditing	Metaevaluation
Proactive: Provide information to improve and monitor the quality of plans and procedures as they unfold.	internal auditor	formative metaevaluator
Retrospective: Attest to overall quality (merit, fairness, dependability, and so forth).	external auditor	summative metaevaluator

External or independent auditors are in private practice or members of public accounting firms and are not employees of the companies whose records and practices they examine. Mautz (1964) explains that internal and external auditors differ on two other important dimensions: (1) Interests served—Internal auditors are not completely independent of management; therefore, their reports or opinions have limited utility to information users (e.g., shareholders, creditors) who must have a report free of management bias or persuasion. In contrast, external auditors market their services on the basis of their independence and objectivity; they are nonstakeholders. (2) Focus of work—Much of the work of external auditors is directed at verifying factual data rather than examining procedures. Internal auditors devote proportionally more time to examining internal operating procedures and practices.

With respect to qualifications, external auditors must first be independent of the auditee and committed to maintaining objectivity throughout the audit. External auditors are CPAs, and, in addition to being technically competent in auditing procedures and accounting methods and practices, they must possess a substantive, working knowledge of the company they are auditing. This substantive knowledge includes understanding the client's organizational structure, accounting policies, product lines, capital structure, and methods of production and distribution (Meigs et al., 1982, p. 107). Furthermore, most external auditors also employ some type of "business approach to auditing" (Taylor & Glezen, 1982), which requires that the auditor be familiar with the general business, industry, and economic issues affecting the auditee. Internal auditors may or may not be CPAs. Their chief qualifications include technical ability, objectivity, and an understanding of their respective company's operations and requirements.

Like his or her financial audit counterpart, a summative metaevaluator (auditor) is expected to be independent of the evaluator/ evaluation and avoid any conflict of interest. It is necessary that he or she be technically competent in evaluation models and methods in general, and highly skilled in the particular methods and techniques employed in the study being examined. It is advisable that he or she possess a working knowledge of the substantive, theoretical, and conceptual issues surrounding the program, project, or product that was the focus of the evaluation being audited. Finally, the summative metaevaluator/auditor should imitate the business approach to financial auditing by seeking an understanding of the factors that led to the evaluation as well as the constraints, limitations, and risks that may have affected the evaluator or the evaluation. (Although there are no current examples that we are aware of, on substantial audits of lengthy or complicated evaluations—i.e., involving multiple methods and theoretical perspectives—we envision the use of audit teams composed of members with different specialities addressing different aspects of the audit work program; see the section on audit work program and work papers). The auditor-auditee and metaevaluator-evaluator relationships create anxiety much like any form of evaluation. Auditors and metaevaluators must strive to form working relationships with auditees based on trust and mutual respect for each other's work.

CHARACTERISTICS OF THE EXAMINATION

Thus far, parallels between auditing and summative metaevaluation have been noted in the parties to an examination, the roles of the examiner, and the reasons for conducting an examination. This section examines the following components of auditing in greater detail:

- Scope and Objectives of an Audit
- Audit Work Program and Work Papers
- Evaluation of Audit Evidence
- Audit Risk and Reliance on Internal Control
- Auditor's Opinion
- Audit Standards

Scope and Objectives of an Audit

Both auditors and metaevaluators must have a clear set of objectives for conducting a particular examination. Schandl (1978) emphasizes that this is a critical requirement:

> Every audit has to have a purpose. The purpose of an audit determines the judgment, the norms to be applied, and the evidence to be used. An audit cannot exist if it has no purpose, and it cannot be good or efficient if it has no well-defined purpose. (p. 173)

These objectives should be negotiated with and agreed to by the auditee and included in the formal contract or letter of agreement prepared at the outset of the audit.

Broadly stated, the objective of an audit of an evaluation is to verify or attest to claims made by the auditee. There are three general classes of claims:

(1) Claims about the evaluation *process*. Examples of these claims include: "The information collected during the evaluation was responsive to the needs of relevant audiences"; "The procedures used to gather and interpret data were reliable, valid, and within the scope of accepted practices"; "The rights of persons participating in the evaluation were protected," and so on.

(2) Claims about the evaluation findings or *product*. Examples of these claims include: "The final report was released in a timely manner"; "The report was disseminated to all responsible parties to the evaluation"; "The report clearly described the evaluand, its context, the purpose of the evaluation, and the findings," and so on.

(3) Claims about both *process and product*. For example, "During the course of the evaluation, steps were taken to enhance the utility of the findings"; "Cost effective procedures were employed"; "Resources were used efficiently during the evaluation"; "Evaluation findings and conclusions are supported in the data," and so on.

The scope of the examination is determined by three factors: (1) the type and number of claims that the metaevaluator (auditor) is called upon to attest to, (2) the particular standards or criteria to be used in evaluating these claims, and (3) the nature and amount of evidence that the auditor must gather to form an opinion. All three of these factors are matters for negotiation between the metaevaluator (auditor) and his or her client (auditee).

Audit Work Program and Work Papers

An audit of an evaluation is a systematic and planned review. It requires a work program that spells out the tasks necessary to accomplish each of the audit objectives as well as time lines for completing each task. This work program is used as a tool for controlling and monitoring audit activities, and it serves as a record of the auditor's examination should the audit itself be questioned.

As an auditor implements the work program, gathers evidence, evaluates it, and forms conclusions, he or she should be preparing a work paper file. According to Meigs et al. (1982), the work papers of an independent, financial auditor should contain the work program, notes, analyses, copies of documents, and so forth; in short, any written records of the work performed by the auditor, the methods or procedures used, and the conclusions reached. We believe that, minimally, the work papers of an audit of an evaluation should contain records documenting the following:

(1) the scope of the audit and the individual audit objectives;
(2) the procedures followed to achieve each objective including sampling strategies and decision rules;
(3) the standards applied to evaluate each claim;
(4) the types of evidence gathered to form an opinion about each claim; and
(5) the completed work program indicating actual time spent on various tasks in the audit.

Work papers are the "connecting link between the audit report and the auditee's records and data" (Holmes & Overmyer, 1976, p. 111). These records document the auditor's methods and conclusions; they are the evidence showing that the auditor's conclusions were reasonable and followed acceptable audit standards (see Chapter 2).

Work papers are prepared at the client's (auditee's) expense, but remain the property of the auditor. In independent, financial auditing, work papers are highly confidential since they often contain information on business plans, benefits and compensation, product profit margins, and other information of a sensitive nature. Their ownership (as property of the independent auditor) has been established by court case (see Holmes & Overmyer, 1976). In cases in which legal action is brought, an auditor may offer the work papers in evidence to support the fairness of audit opinion.

Auditors of evaluation studies are likely to encounter similarly sensitive information in performing an examination, for example actual names of respondents to whom anonymity was promised and given in the final report, the evaluator's personal reflections contained in the field journal, and so forth. Thus maintaining the confidentiality of audit work papers is advisable. The legal ramifications of the use of work papers in metaevaluation at present probably fall within the scope of the obligations and duties that any evaluator currently faces (see, for example, Cahn's [1982] discussion of contracts, general torts, and statutory and constitutional issues).

Evaluation of Audit Evidence

As explained above, an auditor's examination involves verifying assertions made by the auditee. Verification requires the collection and evaluation of evidence, which, as Edds (1980) notes, "is the auditor's stock-in-trade."

The auditor's task is primarily analytical, tracing the work of the auditee to determine whether acceptable practices have been followed and whether conclusions are defensible in view of the data. Evidence is the underlying data, records, and documents that support or corroborate the auditee's assertions. The audit objectives specified for a given audit determine the types of evidence that must be gathered to evaluate the auditee's performance. General types or categories of evidence that might be examined in an audit of an evaluation include the following:

Physical evidence—photographs, videotape or audiotape recordings; raw data files; and so on.

Documentary evidence—interview transcripts and summaries; completed instruments; computer printouts; records of data analyses; written reviews of the literature, reports; and so on.

Internal control evidence—evaluator's log; instructions to interviewers; project scheduling tools; interim or progress reports; evaluation RFP and proposal, written descriptions of procedures; and so on.

Computations—calculations made by the auditor to verify analyses made by the auditee.

TABLE 1.3
Attributes of Audit Evidence

Attribute	Explanation
Relevance	The auditor should avoid wasting time gathering evidence not directly related to the objectives of the audit.
Reliability	Evidence must be competent or trustworthy; it varies in its degree of reliability. The auditor should avoid wasting time gathering and evaluating evidence of doubtful reliability, and instead, seek out more reliable evidence related to the same matter.
Sufficiency	There must be enough evidence to form a valid audit opinion. The auditor must decide when the collective evidence has reached the degree of persuasiveness necessary to permit drawing a conclusion within reasonable limits of risk.
Representativeness	Evidence must be reasonably representative of the whole population of evidence that is under examination.
Timeliness	An auditor must weigh cost and time considerations in gathering additional evidence against the need to deliver a valid opinion in a specified time frame.

SOURCE: Adapted from Edds, 1980, pp. 136-137.

Testimony—oral evidence provided by the evaluator during interviews conducted by the auditor.

With the exception of the last two categories listed above, the client (auditee) provides the evidence for the auditor's examination. The auditee leaves an *audit trail* of evidence that is tracked by the auditor. Chapter 4 illustrates how this very general list of evidential matter is refined in the context of specific audit objectives. It explains the types of evidence that should be included in the audit trail of a naturalistic evaluation.

Auditors use their professional judgment to determine the amount and types of audit evidence required to give a valid opinion. Edds (1980) has discussed the attributes that this evidence must have to be maximally useful to a financial auditor (Table 1.3). The same general attributes characterize the types of evidence gathered in an audit of an evaluation.

The question of how much evidence to gather and evaluate is not easily answered outside the context of a specific set of audit objectives. However, three factors must be considered in making this decision: (1) the amount of time available to conduct the audit, (2) the cost of obtaining the evidence, and (3) the risk of failing to detect some significant (material) error because not enough evidence was gathered. The next section explores these issues of risk and materiality.

Audit Risk and Reliance on Internal Control

In planning and conducting an examination and in forming an opinion, an auditor considers audit risk and materiality. These two notions are interdependent and are considered together in determining how much and what types of evidence to gather and what conclusions to draw on the basis of this evidence. Because financial auditing is an exercise in professional judgment, the auditor runs the risk of being wrong, that is of giving an incorrect opinion on the dependability and fairness of a set of financial statements. Likewise, an auditor of an evaluation runs the risk of giving an incorrect opinion on the merit or quality of an evaluation. Both financial auditors and metaevaluators must be aware of the types of audit risk they face and take steps to minimize those risks.

Risk management has to do with uncovering errors and evaluating them for their materiality. In defining audit risk, the American Institute of Certified Public Accountants (AICPA) (1983, p. 1) emphasizes the relationship between risk and materiality: "Audit risk is the risk that the auditor may unknowingly fail to modify his opinion on financial statements that are materially misstated." In other words, an auditor is at risk in giving an incorrect opinion because he or she failed to detect a material error. A material misstatement or material error is a relative and somewhat nebulous concept. The Financial Accounting Standards Board (1980) defines materiality as follows:

> The omission or misstatement of an item in a financial report is material if, in the light of surrounding circumstances, the magnitude of the item is such that it is probable that the judgment of a reasonable person relying upon the report would have been changed or influenced by the inclusion or correction of the item.

In short, a material error is an error that makes a difference; it is egregious; it is an error that is not inconsequential for understanding the dependability and fairness of a set of financial statements. From a metaevaluator's point of view, a material error in the process of the evaluation is one that could lead to unjustified conclusions; a material error in an evaluation report is one that could mislead the reader or consumer of that report. It is important to realize that neither evaluations nor financial statements are ever completely error free; however, from the point of view of managing audit risk, the issue is not one of uncovering all errors, but errors of substantial significance.

Borrowing from the AICPA's (1983, pp. 7-9) discussion of audit risk and materiality, we have identified three areas of risk wherein metaevaluators acting as auditors must attend to the possibility of material errors. These three include (1) inherent risk, (2) control risk, and (3) detection risk.

Inherent risk. In financial accounting this is the "susceptibility of an account balance or class of transactions to error that could be material. . . . For example, complex calculations are more prone to misstatement than simple transactions; cash is more susceptible to theft than an inventory of coal." Financial auditors must be aware of these potential inherent risks and design their audit work program accordingly.

In an audit of an evaluation, an auditor is advised to attend to inherent risk in aspects of evaluation procedures. For example, it is probable that complex analysis procedures (e.g., cluster analysis, causal modeling) are more susceptible to material error than simple calculations of frequency and mean response; transcribed field notes may be more prone to errors than transcripts of audiotapes; errors in coding and analysis may increase as the number of interviews or surveys increases.

Control risk. This is the risk that a material error "will not be prevented or detected on a timely basis by the system of internal accounting control; that risk is a function of the effectiveness of internal accounting control procedures." A business enterprise establishes a system to control and monitor its operations. This system of controls consists of internal accounting controls—plans and procedures for safeguarding assets and for checking the reliability and accuracy of accounting data—and internal administrative controls—plans and procedures to promote efficiency and encourage adherence to managerial policies (Johnson & Jaenicke, 1980, pp. 7-9). An independent financial auditor is primarily interested in the system of accounting controls, whereas internal auditors are normally concerned with both types of controls (see, for example, Institute of Internal Auditors, 1978).

In performing an independent examination, an auditor may choose to rely on the system of internal accounting controls as a source of evidence after first being satisfied that they are working properly (Meigs et al., 1982). A typical first step in a financial audit procedure is to study and evaluate the system of internal accounting controls through a series of compliance tests to determine if they are working as intended. If the system is weak or not working properly, the auditor must gather greater amounts of other types of evidence.

The notions of internal control and control risk are relevant for audits of evaluations. Every evaluation employs some system for gathering, recording, and analyzing data. In effect, this system is designed to manage data collection, storage, and retrieval and to prevent and detect errors in the evaluation process. The level of complexity of the internal control system will vary with the scope of the evaluation, the number of evaluators involved, and the purpose of the evaluation.

This system of internal control is represented in the audit trail left by the auditee. An auditor of an evaluation study is well-advised to first examine this aspect of the audit trail to determine whether the auditee had in place a mechanism or procedure to guard against errors in the data collection and analysis process. Internal controls for an evaluation might include the following:

(1) a description of the planned design and analysis approaches and any modifications made during the course of the study;
(2) records explaining the role and development of theoretical perspectives;
(3) records indicating procedures and results of pilot tests of instruments; reliability and validity analyses;
(4) records explaining sampling strategies and rationale;
(5) procedures for coding and analysis, including decision rules;
(6) records explaining the system for indexing and cross-referencing data;
(7) the evaluation budget and a record of planned versus actual expenses;
(8) procedures explaining the revision and review of final report drafts; and
(9) procedures for providing anonymity and confidentiality of the data.

Detection risk. This is the risk that financial auditing procedures will not detect a material error. It arises partly because an auditor does not examine 100% of all financial transactions, may have misapplied an appropriate auditing procedure, or selected an inappropriate auditing procedure. Detection risk is managed by a carefully designed audit work program, and (in financial auditing) by a system for supervising and reviewing audit work.

Chapter 2 describes a procedure for auditing aimed at managing detection risk in audits of evaluations. It is our experience that the more carefully planned the audit, the less likely that the auditor will overlook a material error or fail to conduct a thorough audit. Chapter 5 discusses a specific audit procedure in detail.

Finally, it is important to realize that independent, financial auditors do not guarantee that they have discovered and evaluated all material errors. Their opinion provides only reasonable assurance that financial statements are not materially misstated. However, auditors do take every precaution to avoid missing a material error by carefully planning the audit, making a preliminary assessment of risk (assessing audit-ability), and attending to detail in their examination.

Auditor's Opinion

A financial auditor's report does not provide a guarantee or an absolute assurance of the accuracy of a set of financial statements. Rather, the auditor gives information users an informed, professional opinion that the assertions made by the auditee are (or are not) fair and dependable. Meigs et al. (1982) state this situation quite plainly and explain why it is so:

> The auditors cannot guarantee the correctness of the financial statements because the statements themselves are largely matters of opinion rather than of absolute fact. Furthermore, the auditors do not make a complete and detailed examination of all transactions. Their examination is limited to a program of tests that leaves the possibility of some errors going undetected. Because of limitations inherent in the accounting process and because of practical limitations of time and cost in the making of an audit, the auditor's work culminates in the expression of an opinion and not in the issuance of a guarantee of accuracy. (p. 24)

The same conditions obtain for an audit of an evaluation: The evaluation report is largely a matter of opinion (albeit an informed, professional opinion), not fact; the metaevaluator does not review every piece of raw data, examine all field notes, interviews, or completed instruments, or review the logic used by the evaluator in developing and interpreting every analysis scheme; the metaevaluator operates under time and cost constraints; the metaevaluator gives an informed, professional opinion about the trustworthiness of the procedures employed by the evaluator and the conclusions he or she reached. Chapter 3 discusses the issue of an auditor's opinion in more detail.

Audit Standards

This review of shared salient characteristics is not complete without mentioning that both financial audits and audits of evaluations require a set of standards for judging quality. In fact, it is not possible to conduct an audit or metaevaluation without standards, because both activities involve determining the degree of correspondence between assertions made by the auditee (about process and product) and established criteria for performance. The next chapter is devoted to a more complete examination of the use of standards in financial auditing and evaluation.

We can preview the role of standards in evaluation audits and the link between the use of standards and auditing the evaluator's assertions (see the earlier section on "Scope and Objectives of an Audit") by considering the following two examples of how standards might be applied. Imagine that the metaevaluator and his or her client have set the scope of an audit using the Joint Committee's (1981) Evaluation Standards as a guide.

> *Example 1.* Auditor and auditee agree to an audit of the utility of the evaluation. The Standards say that "Utility" means that an evaluation should serve the practical information needs of given audiences. The Joint Committee specifies eight Utility Standards including "audience identification," "information scope and selection," "report clarity," "report timeliness," and "evaluation impact" among others. Thus, to audit for utility, the auditor must gather evidence regarding assertions in three classes. Report timeliness and report clarity are assertions about product; audience identification and information scope and selection are assertions about process, and evaluation impact is an assertion about both process and product.
>
> *Example 2.* Auditor and auditee agree to an audit of the rigor or trustworthiness of an evaluation, and set the scope around the eleven

"Accuracy" standards specified by the Joint Committee. These standards include, among others, "valid measurement," "systematic data control," "justified conclusions," and "objective reporting." To conduct an audit in this case, the auditor must gather evidence to test assertions about process—valid measurement, systematic data control—and process/product—justified conclusions and objective reporting.

In closing, it is important to note that other standards may be used in setting audit scope. The following chapter explains types and uses of standards in greater detail.

SUMMARY

This chapter has defined auditing and illustrated several applications. It has focused attention on analogies between the activities of financial auditing and metaevaluation in three dimensions: the parties to an examination, the role of the examiner, and salient characteristics of the examination.

In general, there are three parties to an audit or metaevaluation: the third-party examiner (auditor or metaevaluator), the client (auditee or evaluator), and users of the audit report (information users or consumers of the evaluation report). Both auditors and metaevaluators can play two roles: a formative, internal, proactive role, and a summative, retrospective, attestation role. For the most part, this book is concerned with the latter. Finally, both auditing and metaevaluation share several characteristics. Both require a clear set of standards and audit objectives, a set of procedures (work program) for achieving those objectives, and work papers documenting that achievement. The central activity of each is collecting evidence to evaluate assertions made by the auditee. Both financial auditing and metaevaluation are exercises of professional judgment and require attention to potential risks and the possibility of material errors.

EXERCISES

1. Discuss the principal qualifications that a summative metaevaluator or external auditor should have.

2. Distinguish between a financial attest audit and an operational audit and compare that distinction to the difference between a formative and a summative metaevaluation.

3. Describe some circumstances in which an independent, third-party meta-evaluator (auditor) might find it difficult to maintain his or her independence.

4. Describe some situations that might create a need for an independent audit of an evaluation study.

2

Differentiating Standards, Procedures, and Accepted Principles

Standard: something established by authority as a rule for the measure of quality;
Procedure: a particular way of accomplishing something;
Principle: a comprehensive and fundamental law, doctrine, or assumption.
                                                    —Webster's, 1983

Standards, principles, and procedures comprise the conceptual framework of an independent financial audit. This chapter extends the
discussion of auditing as a metaphor for metaevaluation by reviewing
this framework in greater detail. Chapter 1 explained that both auditing
and metaevaluation require the use of standards in the act of attesting to
quality. This chapter: (1) explores the definition and use of auditing
standards in greater detail; (2) discusses procedures—the actual steps
taken in conducting an audit; (3) presents a general model for
conducting an audit of an evaluation; and (4) examines the most
problematic of all issues, namely, the issue of accepted principles.

STANDARDS FOR AUDITING AND METAEVALUATION

In financial auditing, auditing *standards* are carefully distinguished
from auditing *procedures*. Auditing standards are rules established by
the American Institute of Certified Public Accountants (AICPA) in the
United States (and the Canadian Institute of Charted Financial
Accountants in Canada) governing the conduct of the auditor and the

quality of the audit itself. Holmes and Burns (1979) define an auditing standard as

> a measurement of performance established by the professional authority and consent of the independent auditing community as a whole. To society, auditing standards represent visible assurance of the quality of various characteristics that should underlie all independent audits. To the audit practitioner, auditing standards represent professional criteria to which an audit must conform. (p. 7)

The Code of Professional Ethics of the AICPA requires that its members abide by what are referred to as generally accepted auditing standards (GAAS). These standards are evidence that the auditing profession is concerned about maintaining uniform, high quality audit work. Table 2.1 displays the standards organized in three areas: (1) general standards, indicating the traits and qualifications that an auditor must possess, (2) field work standards governing the general conduct of the audit, and (3) reporting standards that speak to the nature and content of the auditor's report.

As Meigs et al. (1982) point out, the standards include intangible and ill-defined terms such as "adequately" planned, "sufficient competent" evidential matter, and "proper" evaluation of internal control. This indicates that professional judgment is required in applying the standards. What is adequate, proper, sufficient, and so forth will depend upon the circumstances of each audit examination. The important point here is that auditing standards do not eliminate the need for judgment, rather they provide a framework or set of boundaries within which that judgment is to be exercised.

Generally accepted auditing standards (GAAS) are periodically interpreted and elaborated on by the AICPA's Auditing Standards Board as part of an ongoing effort to enhance and monitor audit quality. Authoritative rulings on auditing standards appear in Statements on Auditing Standards (SAS) (Meigs et al., 1982). SAS No. 1 issued in 1973 complied 54 statements issued by the AICPA in the previous 30 years. Since that time, approximately 40 additional SASs have been issued to deal with new situations and problems. For example, the standards that appear in Table 2.1 were recently refined for specific application to attest engagements (AICPA, 1986). Other Statements have dealt with standards for audit sampling (SAS No. 39), planning and supervision of an audit (SAS No. 22), and evidential matter (SAS No. 31), among other topics.

TABLE 2.1
Generally Accepted Auditing Standards (GAAS)[a]

General Standards

1. The examination is to be performed by a person(s) having adequate technical training and proficiency as an auditor.

2. In all matters relating to the assignment, an independence in mental attitude is to be maintained by the auditor.

3. Due professional care is to be exercised in the performance of the examination and the preparation of the report.

Standards of Field Work

1. The work is to be adequately planned and assistants, if any, are to be properly supervised.

2. There is to be a proper study and evaluation of the existing internal control as a basis for reliance thereon and for the determination of the resultant extent of the tests to which auditing procedures are to be restricted.

3. Sufficient competent evidential matter is to be obtained through inspection, observation, inquiries, and confirmation to afford a reasonable basis for an opinion regarding the financial statements under examination.

Standards of Reporting[b]

1. The report shall state whether the financial statements are presented in accordance with generally accepted accounting principles.

2. The report shall either contain an expression of opinion regarding the financial statements, taken as a whole, or an assertion to the affect that an opinion cannot be expressed. When an overall opinion cannot be expressed, the reasons therefore should be stated. In all cases where an auditor's name is associated with financial statements, the report should contain a clear-cut indication of the character of the auditor's examination, if any, and the degree of responsibility he [or she] is taking.

---

a. Taken from Meigs et al., 1982.
b. Two of the standards of reporting have been omitted because they are not relevant to the practice of evaluation.

Similar auditing standards have also been developed for internal auditors by the Institute of Internal Auditors and for governmental auditors by the U.S. General Accounting Office. All three sets of standards provide professional guidance to the auditor. The standards state requirements and broad procedural guidelines, and each auditing firm or organization must determine how best to achieve those requirements.

In the field of evaluation, several sets of standards have been developed in recent years including those authored by the Joint Committee on Standards for Educational Evaluation (1981), the Evaluation Research Society Standards Committee (ERS Standards Committee, 1982), and the U.S. General Accounting Office (1978). Since metaevaluation is regarded as one of many types of evaluation, these standards are intended to apply to it as well as all other types of evaluation (excluding personnel evaluation, for the present). However, strictly speaking, there are no specific standards that govern the professional conduct of the metaevaluator *qua* metaevalutor in the manner that GAAS speak to the conduct of the independent financial auditor. Evaluation standards are more like accepted accounting principles (see the section "The Issue of Accepted Principles") than auditing standards.

At present, there is probably little need for unique metaevaluation standards because metaevaluators are not accorded the same status or authority vis-à-vis evaluators and consumers of evaluation reports as financial auditors occupy vis-à-vis auditees and information users. Metaevaluation is not a regulated nor highly demanded professional service as is auditing, and special requirements and standards for the practice of metaevaluation are simply not yet an issue.

Should metaevaluation evolve as a service required by evaluators and consumers of evaluation, and should evaluation specialists and the public in general determine that self-regulation and monitoring of the practice is required, it appears that some of the existing evaluation standards could be adapted or translated into something similar to GAAS. For example, GAAS No. 1—an examination is to be performed by person(s) having adequate technical training and proficiency as an auditor—is analogous to a rewording of the Joint Committee's standard for Evaluator Credibility: The person(s) conducting the metaevaluation should be both trustworthy and competent to perform a metaevaluation. Although translating other existing evaluation standards into equivalents of GAAS will not be quite as simple, GAAS can provide a point of departure for developing standards for metaevaluation.

PROCEDURES FOR AUDITING AND METAEVALUATION

In contrast to auditing standards, auditing *procedures* are the specific acts or steps performed by an auditor during an examination to accomplish audit objectives. According to Holmes and Burns (1979, p. 12), audit procedures are "the individual evidence-gathering and evaluation acts performed during the course of an audit." Meigs et al. (1982) provide an example illustrating the difference:

> One of the standards of field work is obtaining *sufficient competent evidential matter* to provide a basis for an opinion. As related to inventory, this standard requires evidence as to quantities and prices of merchandise owned by the client. To meet this standard, the auditors might utilize such auditing *procedures* as (1) observe the taking of physical inventory, (2) compare prices applied to inventory with prices on purchase invoices, and (3) determine that the carrying value of items in inventory does not exceed net realizable value. (p. 23)

A variety of procedures are discussed in the auditing literature and there is considerable room for interpretation on how to combine procedures and apply them to specific audit engagements. Every audit firm has designed its own set of audit procedures. For example, Arthur Andersen & Co. uses a model called Transaction Flow Analysis; Deloitte, Haskins, and Sells use its Study and Evaluation Techniques; Peat Marwick and Mitchell's audit procedures are known as the Systems Evaluation Approach, and Touche Ross's model is called TRACE—Touche Ross Accounting Controls Evaluation. However, the procedures used in each of these models must conform to the guidelines spelled out in the Statements on Auditing Standards noted above.

There are no agreed-upon metaevaluation standards (in the sense of GAAS) that guide the choice and implementation of metaevaluation procedures. However, all of the metaevaluation approaches mentioned in Chapter 1 generally are employed for the same reason, namely, to assess the quality of an original evaluation. Just what constitutes quality is the subject of the next section on "The Issue of Accepted Principles." Since, as we shall see, definitions of quality vary, metaevaluation approaches and procedures vary accordingly.

The remainder of this section extends the analogy between financial auditing and metaevaluation by presenting a general model for auditing evaluations. This model incorporates notions about the audit process that were discussed in Chapter 1. Chapter 5 illustrates how the general model can be expanded and applied to a specific kind of evaluation audit.

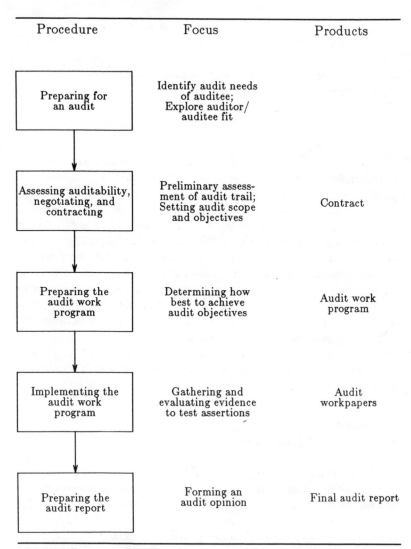

Procedure	Focus	Products
Preparing for an audit	Identify audit needs of auditee; Explore auditor/ auditee fit	
Assessing auditability, negotiating, and contracting	Preliminary assessment of audit trail; Setting audit scope and objectives	Contract
Preparing the audit work program	Determining how best to achieve audit objectives	Audit work program
Implementing the audit work program	Gathering and evaluating evidence to test assertions	Audit workpapers
Preparing the audit report	Forming an audit opinion	Final audit report

Figure 2.1 General Auditing Procedure

Figure 2.1 displays a five-phase general auditing model. The first two phases demonstrate the need for some preliminary work prior to establishing a formal contract or agreement between the auditee and auditor. It is not necessarily the case that the first two phases will comprise two-fifths of the audit either in terms of time or effort; however, this front-end work is extremely important to the overall success of the audit. The heart of the audit process itself is the preparation and implementation of the audit work program along with the writing of the auditor's report.

Preparing for an Audit

The evaluator's decision to audit may result from an agreement with or requirement of the agency sponsoring the evaluation, or it may be a personal goal of the evaluator to demonstrate the quality of his or her evaluation study by having it audited by an independent examiner. If it is known before the study begins that the study will be audited at its conclusion, a statement to that effect and a brief description of the purpose of the audit should be included in the evaluation proposal.

Having made a decision to audit and having contacted an auditor, the auditee should, either verbally or in writing, provide the auditor with background information about the evaluation study. This information may include a description of the context and purpose of the evaluation, the inquiry paradigm or logic of justification employed, the auditee's motivation for having the study audited, the proposed scope and objectives of the audit, and the auditee's expectations of the benefits to be received from the audit.

Assessing Auditability, Negotiating, and Contracting

In the dialogue following the initial request, the auditee and auditor should explore whether the auditor can meet the requirements of the auditee. Factors to be considered in these early negotiations include: (1) auditee awareness of the amount of time required to achieve the proposed audit objectives; (2) auditee awareness of the requirement for an audit trail, (3) auditee requirements regarding the timing and form of the auditor's report; (4) the match between the proposed scope and objectives for the audit and the auditor's capabilities, and (5) any potential conflicts of interest that might impair the independence of the auditor. In these discussions, both auditor and auditee are conducting an auditability assessment as they review and discuss factors that will facilitate, impede, or prohibit an audit examination. These preliminary negotiations should result in either one of two outcomes: (1) the two parties reach an initial agreement pending further auditor orientation or further work by the auditee or (2) they abandon the effort, leaving the evaluator free to seek the services of another auditor or to forgo the audit altogether.

Assuming that the two parties reach an initial agreement, the auditor and auditee then negotiate the scope, objectives, and time required to complete the audit. During these discussions, the auditor must review the structure, substance, and completeness of the audit trail and make a preliminary assessment of inherent and control risk and the overall auditability of the evaluation.

These negotiations conclude with a contract between the two parties specifying: (1) audit scope and objectives, (2) time frame for the audit, (3) any auditee requirements (e.g., preparation or completion of an audit trail), (4) audit fees, and (5) the nature of the deliverable (final audit report). If possible, it is also beneficial to specify criteria for renegotiation in preparation for the unforeseen.

Preparing the Audit Work Program

The auditor's work program specifies procedures to accomplish the agreed-upon audit objectives. He or she develops a work program that describes the evidence to be used in evaluating the auditee's claims about process or product, the criteria or standards for measurement, and the system for filing audit work papers. The intent here is for the auditor to be as explicit about his or her procedures and means for reaching conclusions as the auditee was in conducting the original evaluation. In designing the work program, the auditor carefully considers the issue of detection risk and accordingly develops a thorough and complete set of procedures to fit the circumstances of the audit in question (e.g., claims being made by the auditee, evaluation standards to be applied). Chapter 5 illustrates what a specific audit work program contains.

Implementing the Audit Work Program

During implementation, the auditor actually gathers evidence to evaluate the auditee's claims. The auditor prepares work papers documenting all audit activity and supporting his or her developing opinions. In this phase, if the auditor encounters unanticipated problems in verifying one or more assertions, these problems should be discussed with the auditee and attempts made to resolve them during the audit. For example, the auditor may find that evidence is missing in the audit trail or that the auditee's indexing and cross-referencing system is flawed. The auditor may also encounter more serious problems that are not resolvable during the examination. These may include obvious attempts at deceit (e.g., contradictory data purposefully ignored, data that have been tampered with) or other unethical practices. These issues should also be brought to the auditee's attention to determine whether they are genuine (i.e., confirmable) or the result of auditor misperception. If they are genuine, the auditor must document them and include them in the audit report.

Preparing the Audit Report

The auditor's report should include a brief description of the purpose of the audit, an overview of the audit procedures, a summary of the types of evidence examined, a clear description of the criteria or standards used in making the attestation, and a statement of findings. The statement of findings should clearly express the auditor's opinion on the auditee's assertions (regarding evaluation process and product) that formed the scope and objectives for the examination. Chapter 3 discusses the auditor's report, including types of audit opinions, in more detail.

THE ISSUE OF ACCEPTED PRINCIPLES

In order to judge the quality (understood as fairness and dependability) of a set of financial statements or of an evaluation there must be some generally agreed upon criteria of quality. This section discusses the nature and authority of these criteria in both financial accounting and evaluation. In accounting these criteria are known as generally accepted accounting principles (GAAP); in evaluation these criteria are referred to as evaluation standards.

Accepted Principles in Financial Accounting

Financial statements are audited in view of a set of criteria for quality known as generally accepted accounting principles (or GAAP). It is the

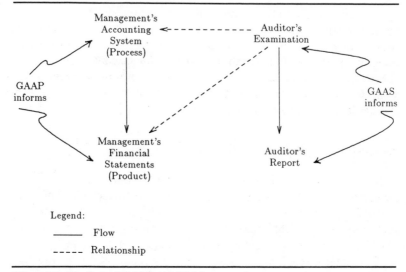

Legend:

——— Flow

- - - - - Relationship

Figure 2.2 The Role of GAAP and GAAS

responsibility of management to use GAAP in recording and processing transactions and in reporting its financial status. These principles are widely know by all CPAs and constitute what is regarded in the profession of accountancy as sound accounting practice. They are recognized as standards for judging auditee performance.

Authoritative pronouncements on accounting principles are issued by the Financial Accounting Standards Board (FASB) and, from time to time, by the Securities and Exchange Commission. The professional effort to establish standards for financial accounting and reporting has a lengthy history. The AICPA began establishing standards through its Committee on Accounting Procedure in 1936. In 1959, pronouncements on standards became the responsibility of another arm of the AICPA known as the Accounting Principles Board. FASB was established in 1973 as the designated organization in the private sector for establishing accounting principles (Financial Accounting Standards Board, 1986). Its seven-member board is assisted by a professional staff drawn from public accounting, academics, government, and industry.

Role of GAAP and GAAS. Figure 2.2 illustrates how accepted principles (i.e., GAAP) and auditing standards (i.e., GAAS) inform the activities of management (the auditee) and the auditor. Management establishes an accounting system (a process) and prepares statements of its financial condition (a product) all in accordance with GAAP. The auditors examine those statements and attest to or verify that they have been prepared and reported in accordance with GAAP. The quality and integrity of the auditor's examination is enhanced by adherence to GAAS during the audit and in the preparation of the audit report. In sum, GAAP are auditee performance standards and GAAS are standards for conducting an audit (Edds, 1980).

Accepted Principles in Evaluation

In the comparatively young field of evaluation, there is no one *authoritative* set of generally accepted evaluation or research principles that defines quality, nor any kind of agency or organization that rules on such standards. As Chelimsky (1983, p. 113) observes in her discussion of defining and measuring evaluation quality for use as a management tool, "there is no clear consensus on the subject . . . definitions are not easy to make because quality is relative to the observer and relative to the conditions imposed on the evaluation being examined." However, there have been several recent attempts to define quality by articulating principles or standards for evaluations.

Chelimsky (1983), for example, reported that, at the Institute for Program Evaluation (now the Program Evaluation and Methodology Division) in the U.S. General Accounting Office (GAO), evaluation quality is defined in terms of technical adequacy and usefulness. Technical adequacy includes three principles: (1) appropriateness of the evaluation design for answering the questions imposed within its time and cost parameters, (2) appropriateness of the evaluation's execution to the design selected and the resources available, and (3) absence of major conceptual errors, inappropriate technical procedures, and improper conclusions or inferences. For each principle, Chelimsky lists a series of questions that managers should ask in order to determine whether the criterion was met. For example, for principle (2) above some of these questions include: How well did the design work? Did staff have problems applying it in the field? Were appropriate statistical tests applied?

The criterion of usefulness is comprised of four principles or standards: (1) relevance of findings to an information need, (2) timeliness of the delivery of findings, (3) presentation quality— organization of the report that is most appropriate to user's needs, and

(4) impact of the evaluation report—"demonstrable use or influence of a report's findings and recommendations in or on legislation, agency decision making, administration, or management."

The Evaluation Research Society (ERS) Standards for Program Evaluation are another attempt to define evaluation quality by describing a set of accepted principles. Prior to the recent merger of the ERS with the Evaluation Network to form the American Evaluation Association (AEA), the ERS Council adopted a set of 55 standards for program evaluation. These ERS Standards (ERS Standards Committee, 1982) are said to be applicable to a wide range of evaluation types including front-end analysis, evaluability assessment, formative evaluation, impact evaluation, program monitoring, and evaluation of evaluation. Expressed in the form of admonitions to evaluators, the ERS Standards cover six components of evaluation activity: formulation and negotiation, structure and design, data collection and preparation, data analysis and interpretation, communication and disclosure, and utilization. Authors of the ERS Standards did not provide illustrations of acceptable practices that might be used to achieve each standard, preferring to let examples of such practices emerge from attempts to apply the standards.

A third, well-publicized, national effort to define standards for evaluation quality is the work of the Joint Committee on Standards for Educational Evaluation (1981). The Joint Committee offers 30 standards as "guiding principles" applicable to evaluations of educational programs, projects, and instructional materials. The Standards are organized into four categories of evaluation quality: (1) utility—an evaluation should serve the practical information needs of a given audience, (2) feasibility—an evaluation should be realistic, prudent, diplomatic, and frugal, (3) propriety—an evaluation should be conducted legally, ethically, and with due regard for the welfare of those involved in the evaluation, as well as those affected by its results, and (4) accuracy—an evaluation should reveal and convey technically adequate information about the features of the object being studied that determine its merit or worth.

Each of the 30 standards is accompanied by a list of "guidelines" or "procedural suggestions intended to help evaluators and their audiences to meet the requirements of the evaluation standard" (p. 16). For example, the standard for "Analysis of Qualitative Information" is: "Qualitative information in an evaluation should be appropriately and systematically analyzed to ensure supportable interpretations." One of the six guidelines for this standard states: "Choose an analysis procedure and method of summarization that is appropriate to the question with which the study is concerned and to the nature of the qualitative information."

Other views of what constitutes quality in evaluations include the GAO (U.S. General Accounting Office, 1978) standards for assessing the impact of social programs, recent efforts by the Joint Committee to establish standards for personnel evaluation (Stufflebeam, 1986), and standards employed by the Auditor General's office in Canada to audit program evaluation studies (Hudson & McRoberts, 1984). We might also be able to synthesize a list of factors defining evaluation quality from Cronbach and his associates' (1980) list of 95 theses.

Several considerations are important in reviewing these attempts to define evaluation principles through standard-setting. Studies have shown that there is a great deal of overlap in the standards (see Cordray, 1982; ERS Standards Committee, 1982; Stufflebeam, 1982). In general, all of the standards speak to the issues of both evaluation process and product by addressing three principles: (1) *rigor* (the right methods properly applied), (2) *value* (the merit, worth, utility, and importance of the evaluation and its findings), and (3) *efficiency-effectiveness* of evaluation planning, implementation, and operations. Despite the overlap, there is no general consensus on the issue of what constitutes acceptable evaluation principles, as evidenced by so many sets of standards. Certainly, there is no one authoritative set of principles nor one governing body that rules on such matters in the practice of evaluation. In the emerging professional practice of evaluation, this is not surprising, given allegiances to different disciplines, paradigmatic debates, and battles over bureaucratic turf. Finally, existing evaluation standards provide macrolevel guidance for conducting evaluations, but little in the way of microlevel guidance. That is, at the level of actual application, there is little agreement on an authority for defining acceptable and nonacceptable practices.

Consider the following example dealing with the principle of evaluation rigor. Of the three dimensions of evaluation quality—rigor, value, and efficiency/effectiveness—rigor has by far had the most scholarly attention. At the macrolevel, all of the standards (each using different language) state that rigor requires (among other things) the use of reliable and valid measurement and appropriate methods of data analysis. But, it is no easy matter to specify, at the microlevel, agreed-upon, accepted practices for establishing reliable and valid measurement and appropriate data analysis. Agreement on accepted practices for documenting rigor is problematic because at least three factors determine acceptability:

(1) *The context of the study.* Time and cost constraints imposed on evaluation studies affect the choice and use of methods to establish rigor.
(2) *The design of the study.* Although concepts of rigor may be analogous across types of designs, different designs require different practices for documenting rigor. For example, compare Goetz and LeCompte's (1984) discussion of accepted practices for reliability and validity in ethnographic design to the discussion by Cook and Campbell (1979) covering quasi-experimental design.
(3) *The logic of justification (inquiry paradigm) employed by the inquirer.* Smith and Heshusius (1986), Lincoln and Guba (1985), Schwandt (1984), and others have shown that the inquiry paradigm that one chooses requires a particular logic of justification that governs what one will regard as acceptable practices for defining aspects of rigor. For example, compare Guba and Lincoln's (Guba, 1981; Lincoln & Guba, 1985, 1986) criteria for establishing rigor to those of Goetz and LeCompte (1984).

Because of the considerable variation in accepted practices attributable to these three factors, it is difficult to define a universal authoritative set of standards at anything other than a macrolevel. Thus, for example, when an evaluator is faced with the task of meeting the Joint Committee's Standard for Analysis of Qualitative Information— "Qualitative information in an evaluation should be appropriately and systematically analyzed to ensure supportable interpretations"—there is considerable latitude involved in defining "appropriate," "systematic," and "supportable."

The principles of and practices for achieving rigor, technical accuracy, or trustworthiness have benefited from decades of attention, yet we still find considerable room for the exercise of professional judgment in defining acceptable practices. We expect even greater variance in the definition and specification of acceptable practices for achieving utility and efficiency/effectiveness—two areas that are relatively far less well defined.

In sum, on the issue of evaluation principles, there are really two distinct but interrelated concerns. The first is the matter of achieving professional consensus on and establishing authority for evaluation standards. Although, as yet, there is no such consensus or authority, there is movement in that direction, particularly via the efforts of the Joint Committee. Second, there is the matter of accepted practices useful in achieving these principles. There are, and likely will always be, differences in accepted practices given different contexts for evaluation, different designs, different values, and different inquiry paradigms. However, this realization does not require that we abandon auditing as a model for metaevaluation. In fact, the situation in financial auditing is somewhat analogous: There we find one set of generally accepted accounting principles but a variety of accepted practices depending upon industry and governmental regulations. Specialized accounting practices and auditing procedures have been designed to meet the requirements of various industries, for example, the oil and gas and financial services industries, and to deal with special issues, for example, leases, repurchase agreements, and financial forecasts and projections. The next section of this chapter reviews the requirements for applying an audit model in metaevaluation.

AUDITING EVALUATIONS

If the situation in metaevaluation were identical to that in financial auditing, we might portray it as shown in Figure 2.3. Evaluators design a study, gather and analyze data (a process), and prepare an evaluation report (a product) in accordance with generally accepted evaluation principles. Metaevaluators audit the evaluation report to attest to or verify that it has been prepared according to generally accepted evaluation principles. The quality and integrity of the audit is assured by the metaevaluator's adherence to standards for metaevaluation.

However, we have seen that there are some important differences in the two professional practices. At present, the practice of evaluation is not yet governed by generally accepted evaluation principles, and the practice of metaevaluation cannot claim to be directed by standards for metaevaluators. It has been noted that divergent views of what constitutes evaluation quality have led to different, though somewhat compatible, standards; at the level of accepted practices a variety of procedures and techniques are possible. In sum, the environment in which evaluation audits are conducted is characterized by (1) multiple evaluation principles, (2) a variety of accepted practices, and (3) different inquiry paradigms and associated designs. Auditing as a

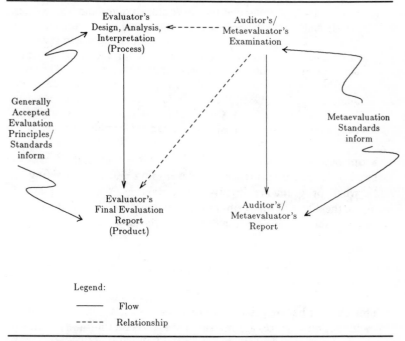

Figure 2.3 The Role of Principles and Standards in Metaevaluation

technique for metaevaluation is applicable in this environment provided that both auditee and auditor carefully attend to the following considerations:

(1) *Scope setting:* Both auditor and auditee must reach agreement on precisely what is to be audited. For example, will the evaluation audit focus on principles of rigor, value, and efficiency/effectiveness? Precisely how, that is, in view of what standards and inquiry paradigms, are these principles to be defined?

(2) *Specification of audit trail requirements:* The scope of the audit will determine the nature and types of evidence that the auditee should assemble in the audit trail. For example, the trail of evidence that an auditor would examine to attest to the efficiency and effectiveness of evaluation procedures would differ from the trail of evidence required to examine whether evaluation procedures and outcomes were rigorous and trustworthy. The auditor's work program would be significantly different in each case as well.

(3) *Specification of evaluation standards:* Both auditor and auditee must clearly understand the criteria or standards that the auditor will use in rendering an attestation. For example, it will not suffice to say that a given evaluation will be (or was) audited for the rigor (technical accuracy, trustworthiness) of its procedures and outcomes. The set of criteria must be specified, i.e., the Accuracy standards defined by the Joint Committee (1981), the criteria for trustworthiness proposed by Lincoln and Guba (1985; Guba, 1981), the criteria for ethnographic design and analysis discussed by Goetz and LeCompte (1984) and so on.

Scope setting, standards specification, and the attendant tasks of assembling a trail of evidence and developing and implementing an audit work program are involved undertakings. Chapters 4 and 5 illustrate these tasks by describing audit trail requirements and an audit work program appropriate to a specific audit scope.

SUMMARY

This chapter has described differences between auditing standards, procedures, and practices as found in financial accounting and examined the practice of metaevaluation in view of the same distinctions. In financial accounting, the term *standards* applies to rules for the conduct of the audit itself; these are known as generally accepted auditing standards, or GAAS. The term *principles* refers to generally accepted accounting principles governing the performance of the auditee, or GAAP. Under the aegis of these principles a variety of accounting practices are permissible. The term *procedures* denotes specific audit procedures.

In the field of evaluation, the term *standards* is used in the same way as the term *principles* is used in financial accounting, namely, as standards for the performance of the evaluation; within these standards a variety of evaluation practices are acceptable. However, evaluation *standards* are not vested with the same authority as GAAP. As regards metaevaluation, strictly speaking, there is no equivalent notion of GAAS, although it is argued that evaluation standards apply to the conduct of metaevaluations.

The chapter also described a five-phase auditing model that can be adapted to fit any special set of circumstances.

EXERCISES

1. Examine the generally accepted auditing standards listed in Table 2.1. Obtain a copy of the Joint Committee Standards (1981). Using the Joint Committee Standards try to develop a list of equivalent auditing standards for metaevaluators. Under what circumstances might it be desirable to have a unique set of standards for metaevaluators?

2. Review the phases in the general auditing model. Imagine that you want to contract for an audit of a recent study you have done. What would you tell the auditor? What would be your audit objectives? What qualifications would an auditor need to audit your study? Place yourself in the role of an auditor for your study and sketch an audit work program to achieve your audit objectives.

3. Explain the following statement: An auditor can use a number of different auditing procedures to determine whether a given evaluation standard has been met.

4. Why are scope-setting and specification of standards for the audit critical to applying an audit strategy to metaevaluation?

5. Obtain a copy of Goetz and LeCompte (1984, Chapter 7), and Lincoln and Guba (1985, Chapter 11), and compare their views of accepted practices for establishing the rigor of an inquiry.

6. Imagine that you are called upon to audit an evaluation to attest to the fact that the evaluator (auditee) met the Joint Committee Standards for Propriety and Feasibility. What types of audit evidence might you need to form an opinion in each situation?

3

Preparing an Audit Report

An audit report is always an expression of an opinion and is not a guarantee.
—Holmes & Burns, 1979

The previous two chapters mentioned some aspects of a final audit report. This chapter examines the form and function of that report in greater detail by considering (1) the elements of a written report, (2) reporting formats, and (3) the auditor's responsibility in issuing a final report.

ELEMENTS OF A WRITTEN FINAL REPORT

In our experience, and in the absence of any standards of reporting on the audit of an evaluation, we have found it useful to include the following six elements in an audit report: report designation/title, statement of purpose, statement of scope, statement of findings (opinion), signature and date, statement of credentials. Each of these elements is discussed below.

Report Designation/Title

The report should be clearly labeled "Independent Auditor's Report" or some other suitable designation. This may seem a trivial point, but it is important in view of the fact that the auditee may include the auditor's report as part of the final evaluation report. The reader clearly should be able to distinguish the evaluation report, as prepared by the auditee, from the audit report, as prepared by the auditor.

Statement of Purpose

Auditees may decide, or be required, to release an audit report to consumers of the evaluation report. Since it is probable that these consumers will not be familiar with an audit approach to metaevaluation, it is advisable that the auditor briefly describe the purpose of conducting an audit of the evaluation in question, the nature of the request for the audit, and the role that the audit played in the study in question. This is particularly critical since an audit can be conducted for a variety of reasons (i.e., to attest to rigor, accuracy, or trustworthiness; to attest to utility, to attest to efficiency and effectiveness, and so on.) The auditor should keep in mind that not all readers of the audit report will be as methodologically sophisticated as the auditee; therefore, it would be wise to avoid using jargon as much as possible. The statement of purpose should clearly identify the auditee, the object being examined (e.g., the final report, the evaluation procedures), and it should provide the dates during which the audit was conducted.

Statement of Scope

The commonly accepted independent financial auditor's short-form report recommended by the AICPA contains a first paragraph that explains the scope of the audit examination:

> We have examined the balance sheet of the XYZ Company as of December 31, 19xx, and the related statements of income, retained earnings, and changes in financial position for the year then ended. Our examination was made in accordance with generally accepted auditing standards and accordingly included such tests of the accounting records and such other auditing procedures as we considered necessary in the circumstances. (Holmes & Overmyer, 1976, p. 10)

The statement of scope in an audit report of an evaluation will never be so brief, but it can serve the same functions. The first sentence in the paragraph shown above clearly states what was examined. A metaevaluator's audit report should do the same. For example, it might say that the audit examined the final evaluation report and the procedures followed by the evaluator in designing and executing the study to enhance the trustworthiness or accuracy of the findings, or it examined the final evaluation report and the procedures used by the evaluator (or evaluation team) to enhance the utility of the findings.

The second sentence of the paragraph displayed above provides readers of the audit report with assurance that the audit was properly conducted. As noted in Chapter 2, metaevaluators do not have an equivalent of GAAS, so it will not suffice to say, "Our (my) examination was made in accordance with generally accepted metaevaluation standards." Unless or until such standards are developed, metaevaluators acting as auditors might provide some assurance to readers of the audit report by making specific reference to the Joint Committee Standards (1981). A brief paragraph could explain that the auditor has read and understands the Joint Committee Standards and has applied them when appropriate in the conduct of the audit.

The second sentence in the short-form report also indicates that, in examining a variety of evidence ("tests of the accounting records and other such auditing procedures"), the auditor has tailored the auditing procedures to satisfy the unique circumstances of the audit in question ("as we considered necessary under the circumstances"). Again, auditors of evaluations cannot afford to be so brief, but they should provide some similar kinds of statements. The types of evidence reviewed in the auditor's examination should be listed. A general description of the audit procedures should be included, and some statement should be made to the affect that audit procedures were tailored to meet the requirements of the particular evaluation and the audit objectives (as described in the previous section).

Statement of Findings (Audit Opinion)

This section of the report should (1) clearly state the auditor's opinion with respect to the auditee's claims in question and (2) indicate the criteria or principles of evaluation that were used in forming that opinion. Several types of opinions are possible, and, as noted in Chapter 2, several sets of evaluation criteria may be used. In attesting to the dependability of financial statements, auditors can render one of four types of opinions—unqualified, qualified, adverse, and a disclaimer of opinion (Holmes & Burns, 1979; Holmes & Overmyer, 1976; Meigs et al., 1982)—in view of the auditee's application of GAAP. The discussion that follows explains how each of these four types of opinions might be used in a metaevaluation audit report.

An *unqualified* opinion is a clean or positive opinion indicating that the auditor has no reservations about the fairness and dependability of the financial statements prepared by the auditee. In the short-form financial audit report noted above, this opinion is succinctly expressed as follows:

> In our opinion, the financial statements referred to above present fairly the financial position of the XYZ Company . . . in conformity with generally accepted accounting principles. . . . (Holmes & Overmyer, 1976, p. 10)

In order to provide both the evaluator and the consumers of the evaluation report with a clear understanding of the results of the audit, an auditor of an evaluation should strive for the same kind of economy of expression. For example, an unqualified metaevaluation audit opinion might read:

> In my opinion, the evaluation report of (name of evaluand) prepared by (name of evaluator) stated the findings fairly and dependably in conformity with the ERS Standards for Formulation and Negotiation, Structure and Design, Data Collection and Preparation, and Data Analysis and Interpretation.
>
> In my opinion, the evaluation of _____ conducted by _____ met the standards for Utility and Feasibility as explained in the Joint Committee Standards for Educational Evaluation.

A *qualified* opinion contains either the phrase "except for" or "subject to." In audits of evaluations, a qualified opinion may be given if the auditee's procedures depart from accepted evaluation principles or standards only in some respect, or if the auditor could not gather sufficient evidence in some area to form an opinion, or if the auditee restricted the auditor's access to information. Examples of these types of qualified opinions include the following:

Situation 1: An evaluation was audited at its conclusion and immediately prior to the release of the final evaluation report. During the course of the audit examination, the auditor accumulated evidence showing that the identity of respondents was not sufficiently protected in the final written report. He or she might issue a qualified opinion that reads:

> Subject to the rewording of the final report currently being performed by the evaluation team, the evaluation of _____ performed by _____ meets the standards for Propriety as spelled out in the Joint Committee's Standards for Educational Evaluation.

Situation 2: An audit is conducted to attest to the accuracy or trustworthiness of six conclusions listed in the final evaluation report. The auditor was unable the trace one of the conclusions completely through the audit trail because critical field notes were missing. The auditor might qualify his or her opinion by saying:

> Except for conclusion number six in the final report (state the conclusion), the evaluation findings regarding (name of evaluand) as prepared by (name of evaluator) are fair and dependable in view of the criteria of dependability and confirmability as described earlier in this report.

It is important to note that before issuing this qualified opinion, the auditor is advised to make every effort to solve the problem of missing evidence by working with the auditee.

Situation 3: An evaluation is being audited against all four sets of the Joint Committee Standards for Evaluations of Educational Programs. During the time period agreed to by the auditee for completing the audit, the auditor was never given access to financial information necessary to form an opinion about the cost effectiveness of procedures and the fiscal responsibility of evaluation management. In this case, assuming that all other standards were met, the auditor would qualify the opinion to express this limitation on his or her examination.

In the examples listed above, a qualified opinion is in order because only certain limitations or exceptions restricted the auditor from issuing a "clean" opinion. In other words, there were several positive conclusions that the auditor felt should be stated, but he or she did have some reservations. When, in the opinion of the auditor, those reservations are of sufficient magnitude to exclude the possibility of a qualified opinion, he or she can render a *disclaimer* of opinion or an *adverse* opinion.

Auditors of evaluation studies would issue a disclaimer of opinion, or a "no opinion" when they believe that they cannot make a judgment of the overall adherence to the evaluation principles in question.

We doubt that a *disclaimer* of opinion would be issued if the auditor and auditee have carefully discussed the nature of the audit, audit objectives, and requirements for the audit trail (see the description of the audit procedure in Chapter 2). However, this opinion is possible if, once the auditor has agreed to conduct an examination, he or she should find the auditee misrepresented the substance and structure of the audit trail. In other words, the trail is so disorganized, incomplete, or inadequate that it cannot be used. Again, we would hope that the auditor and auditee would avoid this situation through careful discussion of the audit trail during the auditability assessment.

The most unfavorable opinion, an *adverse* opinion, would be given when, in the auditor's judgment, the evaluation process or product did *not* meet the evaluation principles or standards being used as criteria. When rendering this opinion, the auditor must carefully explain the reasons why he or she believes that the evaluation did not meet the agreed-upon standards.

Signature and Date

The auditor's report should be signed by the auditor and dated. The date accompanying the signature is the date the audit report was issued. Actual dates during which the audit was conducted should be provided in the Statement of Purpose section of the report.

Statement of Credentials

Unlike financial auditors who are CPAs, metaevaluators do not belong to a society that controls admission, has a professional code of ethics, and establishes minimum requirements for continuing professional education. In short, the appellation of "metaevaluator" attached to an audit report of an evaluation study does not convey a set of credentials as does the designation of "certified public accountant" attached to a signature on a financial audit report. Therefore, it is necessary for metaevaluators to establish their credentials for the readership of the audit report. This can be accomplished by appending to the report a brief resume that reviews the metaevaluator's qualifications in both methodological and substantive areas.

REPORTING FORMATS

As described in the general auditing model presented in Chapter 2, the types of audit reports should be negotiated and specified in the audit contract. This section discusses several reporting options that auditees and auditors might consider.

An auditor of an evaluation study should issue a final written report, but that does not preclude additional ways of reporting audit results. Independent financial auditors often make a presentation of their findings to a client's audit committee, and operational and management auditors are advised to review their findings with management prior to issuing a final report. This kind of reporting signifies that financial auditors are not simply watchdogs or policemen, but management consultants who offer professional opinions on their clients' business operations and who have a genuine interest in assisting their clients.

In an audit of an evaluation, a prerelease draft of the final audit report may be given to the auditee. In the field of management auditing, Edds (1980) explains that this practice can be used as a means to resolve client conflicts, reach agreement on facts, permit the auditee to see in advance the written word, and to ensure the auditee's proper consideration of the auditor's findings.

An oral report of findings to the auditee can also be made prior to the issuance of the final report. This situation might be regarded as a briefing in which the auditor presents the format of the final report and reviews the statement of purpose and the audit opinion. Any disagreements arising between the two parties can be resolved at the conclusion of the briefing. To facilitate the discussion and to make the best use of available time, the auditor is well-advised to prepare carefully for the briefing.

At the auditee's request, an oral briefing on audit findings might be made to consumers of the evaluation report. If this briefing is made as part of the auditee's presentation of evaluation findings, the auditor should make it clear that he or she is delivering an independent, third-party opinion of evaluation quality. The auditor should also be prepared to comment on his or her qualifications, procedures, and the standards used to attest to quality.

Finally, following an occasional practice in financial auditing (Holmes & Burns, 1979), it may be desirable to issue both a short-form and long-form auditor's report. In financial auditing, a short-form report is a basic two paragraph opinion accompanying the financial statements. If readers have ever seen a company's annual report to its stockholders, they have seen this short-form auditor's report. A more detailed, long-form report may also be prepared for management's use. Auditors of evaluations may find it useful to follow a similar practice: an abbreviated, short-form report to be attached to the evaluator's final evaluation report, and a more detailed, long-form report to be shared with the evaluator and distributed at his or her discretion. Auditees might supply a short-form auditor's report in their executive summary of a lengthy study and include a long-form in the more detailed technical report of the evaluation.

A Comment About Standardized Reports

We wish to add one caveat concerning the development and use of standardized audit reports to this discussion of the form and content of reports. Comments about the need for clarity in the written report and examples of statements that might be contained in an auditor's report should not be taken to mean that auditors of evaluation reports should strive for a standardized reporting format. On the contrary, although it would be useful if all reports exhibited a similar structure (i.e., contained the six elements described above) the actual content of each report can and should meet the specific requirements and needs in each audit situation.

To be sure, it is unlikely at present that the practice of auditing evaluations will resort to standard report forms. However, it is instructive to note the experience of the profession of accounting on this issue. The possibility that standardized reporting is contributing to the growing perception gap between auditors and information users has been a topic for consideration in the accounting and auditing profession for the last decade. Mednick (1986), for example, cites the work of the AICPA's Cohen Commission, which concluded that the standardized short-form audit report has contributed to the public's misunderstanding of the auditor's role and responsibilities. The Commission observed that

> one effect of using a standard report is that as a person becomes familiar with its words, he tends to stop reading it each time he sees it. . . . The

attempt to communicate separate messages becomes less successful as a reader becomes more familiar with the standard language. (cited in Mednick, 1986, p. 71)

The Commission explained that although auditors assume the following conditions of the examination, the actual report does not clearly communicate them to the reader: that the financial statements are prepared by management; that the auditor examines management's use of accounting principles that are appropriate in the circumstances; and that the auditor used professional judgment in forming an opinion. In view of the experience of the financial auditing profession, auditors of evaluation studies are well-advised to communicate clearly their role and responsibilities to auditees and consumers of evaluation reports.

THE AUDITOR'S RESPONSIBILITY

In conducting an examination and preparing an audit report, an auditor assumes several responsibilities vis-à-vis both the auditee and consumers of the evaluation report. This section describes some of these ethical dimensions of the auditor's role.

First, the auditor acting in a summative metaevaluator role must clearly communicate to the auditee and consumers of the evaluation report that the conduct of the actual evaluation, including all procedures and reporting, is the responsibility of the auditee. Although the auditor attests to the auditee's assertions (as explained in Chapter 1), he or she does not make those assertions. We can reiterate the role of an auditor that was presented in Chapter 1 by emphasizing with Edds (1980, p. 5) that the purpose of an audit is to "enhance the value of information already prepared by the auditee; it does this by adding credibility to the auditee's information."

Second, auditors also have the responsibility of explaining to parties involved in the audit that the auditor is not conducting the audit for the purpose of uncovering unethical or fraudulent behavior on the part of the auditee. Much like a financial attest audit (see American Institute of Certified Public Accountants, 1977), an audit of an evaluation is not designed to detect this kind of behavior. Of course, if an auditor has evidence to support a finding of unethical behavior, he or she cannot simply ignore it. At minimum, the auditor should discuss the matter with the auditee. If it cannot be satisfactorily resolved, we would assume that an auditor would render an opinion accordingly.

Defining unethical behavior in evaluation is no simple task and is beyond the scope of this introduction to metaevaluation as auditing. Readers interested in pursuing this topic further are invited to review the papers presented at the symposium on Ethical Issues in Evaluative Research at the 1986 annual meeting of the American Educational Research Association (see, for example, Stufflebeam, 1986; Strike, 1986); papers from a symposium at the same conference on Ethical Concerns in Qualitative Research (see, for example, Flinders, 1986; Thornton, 1986; Besag, 1986), or more lengthy treatments of the issues (for example, Diener & Crandall, 1978; Cassell & Wax, 1980). For a general discussion of the legal liabilities of financial auditors see, for example, Meigs et al. (1982). For an overview of legal considerations involved in program evaluation see Thurston, Ory, Mayberry, and Braskamp (1984).

Third, the auditor has the responsibility of explaining to all parties involved in an evaluation audit that he or she is examining the use of evaluation principles and practices that the *auditee* considers appropriate in the circumstances. In other words, the auditor is not responsible for the choice of a particular set of practices to achieve evaluation principles or standards. Auditors attest to the fact that the auditee's practices are (or are not) within the generally broad boundaries of sound practice. They are obliged to document opinions to that effect by reference to the audit work papers, and they must be capable of demonstrating that they acted reasonably and competently in reaching those opinions.

Fourth, the auditor must always emphasize that the independent audit report is a professional opinion on, not a guarantee of, quality. Should Stufflebeam's (1986) advice to the profession to increase third-party audits of evaluations be acted upon, metaevaluators can learn valuable lessons from the current perception gap between financial auditors and users of their reports (see, for example, Mednick, 1986; Reichner, 1986; Gaines, 1986; "Accountants stray," 1985).

Finally, the auditor should attend to the issue of independence in the evaluator-auditor-evaluation consumer relationship. He or she should thoroughly explore the possibility of conflict of interest before contracting to perform an audit and maintain independence during the audit.

SUMMARY

This chapter has discussed aspects of the preparation and presentation of an auditor's report. It identified six elements that an audit report should contain, including the report designation/title, the statement of purpose, the statement of scope, the statement of findings, and the signature/date. Oral and written options in audit reporting were reviewed, and the chapter concluded with a brief discussion of the auditor's role and responsibilities to the other parties involved in an audit examination.

EXERCISES

1. Review the discussion of qualified opinions and discuss other circumstances that may lead to this kind of opinion.

2. In the absence of any specific standards for metaevaluators acting as auditors, how can auditors provide assurances concerning their work? What actions can they take to merit confidence in the audit opinion?

3. Imagine that you are asked to present an audit report to parties with a vested interest in an evaluation. What steps would you take in preparing for the report? How would you organize the presentation? Would your organization differ if the report contained a qualified opinion? Explain.

4. Imagine that you are a consumer of an evaluation report (a member of the policy-shaping community). What would assure you that the audit examination of that report was trustworthy? What characteristics of the auditor would you look for? What information would you want to see in the final audit report?

4

Constructing an Audit Trail

BACKGROUND TO THE ILLUSTRATION

Chapters 4 and 5 present auditing in the context of attesting to whether a naturalistic inquiry has met criteria for trustworthiness (Guba & Lincoln, 1981; Lincoln & Guba, 1985). As a methodological paradigm, naturalistic inquiry can be applied to a variety of inquiry situations including research, evaluation, and policy analysis (Lincoln & Guba, 1985, p. 226). Our particular illustration deals specifically with naturalistic inquiries having a focus on an evaluand; however, the information presented in Chapters 4 and 5 could be applied with minor modifications to other inquiry situations as well.

Readers with limited familiarity with naturalistic inquiry are encouraged to examine the methodology (Guba, 1978, 1981; Guba & Lincoln, 1981; Lincoln & Guba, 1985, 1986; Williams, 1986). A brief review of salient considerations follows as background to the next two chapters: As a means of establishing or verifying the rigor or trustworthiness of naturalistic inquiries, Guba and Lincoln (Guba, 1981; Lincoln & Guba, 1985, 1986) have proposed a set of criteria analogous to conventional notions of internal and external validity, reliability, and objectivity. These criteria include:

(1) *Dependability* (analogue to reliability): This is a criterion of consistency. It is concerned with the process of the inquiry. It emphasizes that the procedures employed in a naturalistic inquiry should fall within generally accepted practice and be carefully documented.
(2) *Confirmability* (analogue to objectivity): This is a criterion of neutrality. It is concerned with the product or outcomes of an inquiry. It emphasizes that interpretations should be grounded in the data and formulated in ways consistent with the available data.

(3) *Credibility* (analogue to internal validity): This is a criterion of "truth value." It emphasizes that findings and interpretations arrived at via naturalistic inquiry should be perceived as credible by those respondents who supplied the original data.

(4) *Transferability* (analogue to external validity): This is a criterion of applicability. It is virtually a moot issue in naturalistic inquiry for, as Lincoln and Guba (1985, p. 316) explain, "The naturalist cannot specify the external validity of an inquiry; he or she can provide only the thick description necessary to enable someone interested in making a transfer [of findings] to reach a conclusion about whether transfer can be contemplated as a possibility."

For each of these criteria, Lincoln and Guba have specified a variety of techniques useful in increasing the likelihood that they will be met or to test whether they actually have been met. Of primary concern for our purposes is that Guba (1978, 1981) has proposed auditing as a principal means of establishing whether criteria of dependability and confirmability have been achieved. One of the authors (Halpern, 1983) first operationalized this particular approach to auditing. He found that in addition to attesting to dependability and confirmability, the audit strategy could be used to gather information for verifying whether the criterion of credibility had been appropriately addressed in a naturalistic inquiry.

This, then, is the context in which the following two chapters are written. This chapter discusses the form and substance of an audit trail that a naturalistic evaluator (auditee) would assemble in anticipation of having his or her evaluation audited for dependability and confirmability. Chapter 5 presents an audit work program that an auditor (metaevaluator) might follow in auditing a naturalistic evaluation against these criteria. These chapters assume that readers are familiar with issues and methods in qualitative data analysis; relevant references are provided for additional information. Much of what is presented in these chapters has applicability beyond the naturalistic inquiry paradigm, and that is the subject of Chapter 6.

We have chosen this particular illustration for two reasons. First, these kinds of studies, as compared to more conventional approaches to evaluation, are often viewed as weak in demonstrating rigor, technical accuracy, or trustworthiness (see, for example, Miles & Huberman, 1984). As advocates of this approach to inquiry, we would like to bolster its defensibility. Therefore, the audit trail and audit work program described here and in Chapter 5 are not only examples of the application of auditing philosophy to metaevaluation, but also a means for evaluators who use naturalistic or interpretive inquiry to review and monitor the integrity of their work as it unfolds. Second, we believe that auditing rigor, technical accuracy, or trustworthiness in naturalistic inquiries is one of the more complicated and challenging applications of an auditing approach. If it can be shown that an auditing strategy is workable in this situation, then readers may be encouraged to try their hand at developing an audit model in other circumstances (e.g., auditing for utility) and with other evaluation methodologies (e.g., quasi-experimental designs).

INTRODUCTION

This chapter is written for an evaluator (auditee) who plans to prepare an audit trail to document the rigor or trustworthiness of a naturalistic evaluation. The first part of this chapter presents a general four-stage procedure for preparing an audit trail and discusses the auditee's tasks and resulting products. The second part of the chapter takes an in-depth look at a number of possible audit trail files and records that may be generated by the auditee. This discussion will also describe what the auditor will look for in the audit trail when conducting the audit. Throughout this chapter, *auditee, evaluator,* and *inquirer* are regarded as synonymous, as are the terms *auditor* and *metaevaluator.* The term *inquiry* refers to an inquiry wherein the focus is an evaluand.

Preparing an audit trail is important for two reasons. First, it documents the inquiry in a fashion that facilitates a third-party examination. The audit trail contains information that describes the methods used to control error and to reach justifiable conclusions. Second, an audit trail is also important for the evaluator. We have found that when auditees systematically document their inquiries in anticipation of an audit, it helps them manage their record keeping (Halpern, 1983; Covert & Stahlman, 1984). They find an organized trail useful when they need to retrieve information easily and when they prepare their final reports. Some auditees have suggested that when they document each inquiry decision, they become more thoughtful, critical, and reflective.

A systematically kept documentation system will serve a quality control function during an evaluation and will help guide the evaluation process in accord with generally accepted evaluation principles. As noted in Chapter 1, a system of record keeping and documentation prepared for an evaluation is analogous to the internal control

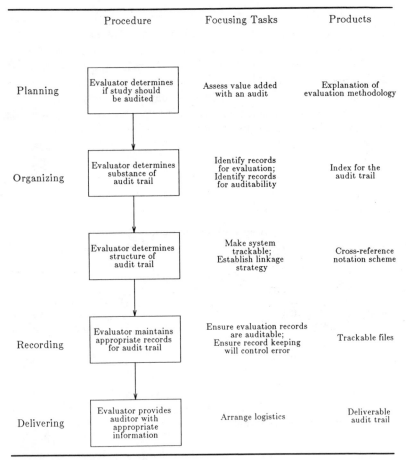

Figure 4.1 Preparing an Audit Trail

mechanism for managing business operations. By establishing a basic controlling mechanism and adhering to policies and procedures, a business organization attempts to prevent and detect errors in its accounting and financial reporting systems. Similarly, internal controls for an inquiry make it more likely that the inquirer will document decisions and follow acceptable evaluation practices. From the auditor's perspective, an appraisal of the internal control mechanism itself is an initial goal. The auditor will form an opinion about the design and implementation of the auditee's mechanism for controlling and minimizing errors in the evaluation.

PREPARING AN AUDIT TRAIL

Figure 4.1 illustrates a simple four-stage model for planning, organizing, recording, and delivering an audit trail. Each stage is described below.

Planning

As part of planning for the evaluation, evaluators are advised, whenever possible, to determine whether an audit is desirable or necessary, that is, whether it will add value to the evaluation. If an audit is called for, evaluators can incorporate plans for assembling the audit trail into their overall evaluation plans. In other words, they can consider what kinds of documentation will be prepared and maintained for the auditor's examination, and how it will be prepared and maintained. From an auditor's point of view, a planned audit trail is preferable to a trail of evidence that is reconstructed once the evaluation is underway. A planned trail is more likely to contain all of the necessary materials.

Organizing

Once the decision is made to be audited, or at least to design the records with an audit in mind, the evaluator should determine what records will be kept (audit trail substance) and how they will be filed (audit trail structure). Evaluators must decide whether the record-keeping systems they normally maintain will facilitate an audit, and, if not, how they must be modified. Even when the files are not optimal for an audit, an audit can be conducted. However, it is likely that the examination will take longer to complete, and the audit costs as well as the risk of failing to detect errors may increase. In nonaudited evaluations, record-keeping systems often do not include records of decisions and decision rules, changes in methodology, cross-references to all other notes, an index that serves as a key to understanding the cross-reference scheme, and explanations showing how data were reduced. These file types are important to enabling an audit and will be discussed later in this chapter.

Recording

Once the inquiry begins, the evaluator builds an audit trail by keeping records and filing them into a well-organized system. These records should not only facilitate an audit but also contribute to the management of the inquiry. If the evaluator's records and documentation system are prepared to accomplish only the former, then he or she is likely to be complying with the letter but not the intent of the audit approach to quality control. Accurate and complete records of a naturalistic evaluation must be viewed as a means of improving the quality of the evaluation as it unfolds as well as an avenue for the review of quality after the fact. Inquirers unaccustomed to keeping detailed records may find this task of documenting research-in-use initially daunting (and onerous). Yet, the task is not unreasonable, and it has considerable payoffs. We do not advocate a focus on auditability during the evaluation if it detracts from the more important issue of ensuring timely completion of a rigorous study. Evaluators will have to learn to strike an appropriate balance between their own inquiry needs and the needs of the auditor.

Delivering

At an agreed-upon time, the evaluator will provide the auditor with access to the audit trail. In some cases, it may be desirable or necessary for the evaluator to remain available to answer questions. The role the evaluator plays after providing the auditor with access to the records should be negotiated.

AUDIT TRAIL ELEMENTS

Having looked at these few general steps required in preparing an audit trail, we will next look at specifications for what an audit trail might contain. The remainder of this chapter will describe some ways that auditees can prepare internal control systems by documenting their methods. It will focus on how to represent decisions, data collection, and data analysis strategies in written records in a way that enhances both quality control and auditability.

Explicit records about the emerging evaluation design will provide trackable evidence of the auditee's internal controls. The auditor will look for illustrations of the inquiry processes and the resulting products; evidence of the auditee's lines of thinking and self-evaluations about the inquiry, and subtle influences of the auditee's fears and introspections about using various methods. In essence, the auditor will expect to see a "thick description" not only of the inquiry context, as described by Geertz (1973), but also of the inquiry process.

Record-Keeping System

There are many ways to manage a naturalistic inquiry through the documentation. Systems have been recommended by Schatzman and Strauss (1973), Corsaro (1981), Bogdan and Biklen (1982), Lincoln and Guba (1985), and Lofland, (1971). For example, Corsaro (1981) and Schatzman and Strauss (1973) recommend keeping four types of notes: (1) *field notes* that include descriptions of the content and context and are normally derived from interviews and observations; (2) *methodological notes* that describe all ongoing methodological decisions and methodological shifts, including sampling decisions and interview strategies; (3) *theoretical notes* that describe the evolving theory, including working hypotheses and evolving category structures; and (4) *personal notes* that contain records of feelings and intuitions and often serve a cathartic function for the inquirer.

In a similar vein, Bogdan and Biklen (1982) recommend using field notes and reflections. The reflections are subjective and should include all thoughts and feelings about methods, analysis, ethical issues, personal frame of mind, and so forth. Lofland (1971, p. 106) also suggests that raw field notes be supplemented by basic analytic ideas and inferences, no matter how "far-fetched and wild" they may seem. He also recommends recording personal impressions and feelings as a means to be "privately honest with oneself about one's feelings." Lincoln and Guba (1985, p. 327) suggest keeping a "reflexive journal." Referring to the inquirer as a "human instrument," they suggest that this diarylike journal maintain data about "self." They also advocate using this journal to keep records of the daily schedule, cathartic and reflective notes, and a methodological log.

Although these strategies for documenting inquiries were advanced to instruct a field researcher, we have found them worthwhile to incorporate into a scheme for the forms and types of records and files that should be part of an audit trail for a naturalistic evaluation. What differs is the notion that these records would be reviewed by a third party. In general, for a good audit trail, we recommend that the naturalistic evaluator keep the types of records described above, and organize them in such a way that will make it possible for the auditor to be able to "replay" any portion of the inquiry. With this goal in mind, we will look first at the basic substantive requirements of an audit trail, and then at the basic structural or organizational considerations. This will be followed in the second half of this chapter with a detailed discussion of recommendations for constructing an audit trail in a naturalistic evaluation.

Substantive Items

As discussed in Chapter 2, a financial audit trail contains such standard items as physical evidence, documentary evidence, internal control evidence, computations, and testimony. These items enable an auditor to verify the claims of the auditee. In an audit of a naturalistic evaluation, in order for an auditor to verify assertions, the audit trail must contain items that reflect the inquiry process. When we examine the tasks involved in a naturalistic evaluation, we find there are four areas in which files may be kept: (1) *evaluation plans;* (2) *events under study;* (3) *evaluator behaviors;* and (4) *evaluator thoughts and feelings.* How each of these is represented is a matter of individual preference. Each of these types of information will be explained briefly below. The last part of the chapter will describe one strategy for developing a comprehensive audit trail incorporating these types of files.

Evaluation Plans

Evaluation plans refer to information normally contained in an evaluation proposal, including proposed methodology and relevant background theory, literature, or prior investigative work. The methodological information will normally describe what data collection and analysis techniques were planned, and why and how rigor was designed into the evaluation. If the evaluation was based on any prior work, the auditor should be given access to the evaluator's assessment of that work in order to gain insight into predispositions of the evaluator.

Events Under Study

These "events" refer to that which the evaluator studied (i.e, the evaluand, the context, setting, and so on). They will be portrayed in three forms—as raw data, as transformed data, and as findings. Naturally, raw data files are kept for every evaluation and are not prepared solely for the audit. Since they will not be displayed in a final evaluation report, the auditor will need to obtain access to these raw data files in order to make judgments about them for the benefit of the report readers. For the auditor to accomplish this efficiently, the evaluator should organize the data files with the expectation that an auditor will use them as evidence in attesting to the confirmability of the inquiry (Guba, 1981; Halpern, 1983).

Transformed data files will show the ongoing efforts of the evaluator to reduce and reconstruct the data into an evolving interpretation. For example, these files should contain copies of diagrams and data displays showing how initial depictions of relationships among categories of data were refined into charts and tables. These files will show the lines of thinking of the evaluator, particularly how he or she prioritized information. For example, if after analyzing the data, the evaluator decided to exclude some findings from the final report, they would still appear in the audit trail thereby allowing the auditor to examine what the evaluator (auditee) chose to emphasize and what was downplayed.

Evaluator Behaviors

Records of these "behaviors" explain what the evaluator did, when, and why. Ideally, each methodological or procedural decision is logged for the record in much the same way that the evaluator would record raw data about substantive issues. Information about changes in procedures or methods during the study (characteristic of a naturalistic evaluation) is crucial for the audit. This information is not likely to be found in a final report because these shifts may occur so frequently that they would create excessive detail in a final report. These audit trail entries should illustrate the responsive nature of the evaluation, the rationale for theoretical or purposeful sampling decisions, and how each method-ological decision was tied to the emerging interpretation and working hypotheses. As with the events under study, the evaluator should organize these data files with the expectation that they will be used as evidence in attesting to the dependability of the inquiry (Guba, 1981; Halpern, 1983).

Evaluator Thoughts and Feelings

The audit trail should show the personal side of the evaluator as well as information about the psychology behind data reduction. The personal, diarylike entries should display the reflective nature of the evaluator; his or her feelings, biases, hunches, wild guesses, and thoughts about the evaluation. We cannot overemphasize the importance of the practice of writing down feelings, ideas, reactions, and speculations during the evaluation. This practice serves to keep ideas flowing, to promote further insights, and to reflect on the field experience (Lofland, 1971; Glaser & Strauss, 1967). By writing these notes, the evaluator taps into his or her own tacit knowledge, fully exploiting the unique power of the human as research instrument.

The cognitive aspects of data reduction should also be described in the diary or reflexive log kept by the evaluator. The way in which the evaluator processes and filters information and the underlying decisions (conscious or unconscious) that go into developing an interpretation should be described. The evaluator should document, minimally, the *rules* used for inclusion/exclusion of information, how data were *reduced*, and how data were *recombined*. This information will help the auditor gauge how systematically rules were applied during data reduction.

Structural Considerations

Depending on its size and resources, a business will assemble the items in a financial audit trail in some type of paper or electronic filing system. In a naturalistic evaluation, the auditee must also consider a system that enables tracking. Regardless of the storage medium, the following four structural considerations are proposed: (1) *filing system,* (2) *cross-references,* (3) *indexes,* and (4) *dates.*

Filing System

Because large amounts of data and records typically are generated during a naturalistic evaluation, a well-organized filing system is helpful to the evaluator as well as to the auditor. Lofland (1971, p. 118) suggests that interview (or field) notes be filed into a "flexible storage, ordering, and retrieval format" and that multiple copies be made to permit filing in more than one category. Levine (1985) recommends a data storage and retrieval system that is thoughtfully formatted, cross-referenced, indexed, abstracted, and paginated. The interested reader is referred to Levine's article as well as to Miles and Huberman's (1984) book for a variety of strategies useful for filing, organizing, and displaying qualitative data. The evaluator must decide whether to organize data into files by interview, by topic, by issue, or chronologically. He or she must determine whether folders, electronic storage, file cards, or other types of physical storage will be used. Whatever system is developed, sorting and filing must be meaningful to the study and useful to the evaluator.

Cross-References

Each record, each page, and each significant item should be marked with a unique identifier that documents from what other record(s) it was derived. When raw data are interview records, they should contain either the name of the respondent or a code number or letter. It might also be helpful to number the paragraphs or significant statements. Reduced data items should contain the respondent's name or code identifying the interview record it came from, and a code that points to the exact section of the raw data record (for example, the paragraph number). Similarly, when categories of data are formed, they should display a code that maps to codes entered on both the reduced and raw data. In this way an auditor will be able to select a finding and track it to all other relevant audit trail records.

Indexes

Index pages should provide a high-level view of the organization of the filing system. Where relevant, they should also provide a high-level view of the coding scheme used in the cross references. The index should contain a list of all file names, the contents of each file, and the code number used to reference that file.

Dates

Each record should be marked with the date of entry, and the date of the event if they differ. This will enable both the auditor and the evaluator to recreate a sequence of events and decisions in the study at any point in time.

Inclusiveness and Organization of the Audit Trail

As implied in the previous sections, the audit can best occur when there is sufficient documentation. The audit will be conducted efficiently only when the existing documentation is organized in a fashion that facilitates tracking across the records. If there is insufficient documentation, the missing information may not be retrievable after the study is completed. If the records are not organized to assist tracking, the auditee may be able to insert the necessary cross-references after the fact, but only with a great deal of effort. Adding cross-references after the fact requires working through numerous pages and records and increases the probability of making errors.

We hesitate to be overly prescriptive on audit trail requirements because we do not want them to intrude on the procedures that an evaluator might otherwise follow, or on the records that he or she might normally keep. We also want to emphasize that an evaluation low on auditability requirements does not imply an *inadequacy* of the evaluation. We *do* want to emphasize that when an audit trail is less than optimal, the auditor will experience difficulty when tracking, the audit will be less timely, more expensive, or impossible to conduct altogether. An inability to audit does not imply that the study itself is not rigorous. It *does* imply that other methods of determining quality or rigor may have to be employed. The remainder of this chapter discusses the many kinds of records that can be kept, and how they contribute to enabling an audit. Table 4.1 displays a general organizational framework for documenting a naturalistic evaluation and is explained on the following pages.

The audit trail framework or scheme presented in the remainder of this chapter categorizes files in a logical sequence. This framework should be viewed as a list of possibilities for record keeping. Highly structured record keeping is important to naturalistic evaluation because the evaluator is an integral and potentially undisciplined biasing force during data collection. Therefore, the auditee (evaluator) must document in a structured way the thoughts and otherwise hidden decisions that drive the direction of the evaluation both methodologically and theoretically. Table 4.1 (Files and Forms of Inquiry Documentation) displays various types of records. We do not plan to discuss the pros and cons of different methods from any inquiry standpoint, or the rules of data collection and analysis. We will focus on ways of representing information to facilitate an auditor's job, leaving the methodological and tactical details of data collection and analysis to others who have written comprehensive and detailed discussions, for example, Gorden (1975), Becker (1970), Patton (1980), Spradley (1979), Miles and Huberman (1984).

The first column of Table 4.1 identifies six audit trail file types. The first three—*raw data files, data reduction files,* and *data reconstruction*

TABLE 4.1
Files and Forms of Inquiry Documentation

File Types	Forms of Data	Examples
Representing Phenomena		
1. raw data files	A. unfiltered accounts	• descriptions of evaluand, descriptions of phenomena, events, behaviors, social interactions, & feelings
	1. videotapes (and transcripts)	
	2. audiotapes (and transcripts)	
	3. photographs	• flow of operations; test scores; organizational histories; memos
	B. filtered accounts	
	1. unobtrusive accounts	
	a. stenomask records	
	b. observational records	• physical design charts; time series photographs
	c. documents & existing records	• referential adequacy materials
	d. notes on physical traces	
	2. interactive accounts	
	a. interview notes & writeups	
	b. survey results	
2. data reduction files	A. summaries of raw data	• personal accounts
	1. condensed notes	• events
	2. writeups	• quotes
	3. units of information/categories	• social interactions
	4. data displays and tally sheets	• themes
	5. computer analysis summaries	• behavior patterns
		• concerns

(continued)

TABLE 4.1 Continued

File Types	Forms of Data	Examples

3. data reconstruction files	A. theoretical notes
	  1. working hypotheses
	  2. lists of novel concepts
	  3. hunches and insights
	B. relationships among categories
	  1. themes
	  2. definitions
	  3. relationships
	C. findings and conclusions
	D. reports
	  1. draft report(s)
	  2. final report
		• relationships between concepts and categories
		• explanations of concepts, themes, and categories
		• inferences and interpretations
		• connections to existing literature; to other evaluands
		• integration of concepts and methods

Representing Inquiry Procedures		

4. process notes (methods)	A. methodological notes
	  1. procedures
	  2. strategies
	  3. day-to-day decisions and rationale
	B. notes about trustworthiness
	  1. credibility methods
	  2. dependability methods
		• lists of daily activities
		• decision-making rules
		• sampling techniques
		• descriptions of emerging design
		• explanation of data reduction strategy
		• instrument development selection process
		• notes about peer debriefing interactions

3. confirmability methods
   - member check strategy, interactions and results
   - triangulation strategy and results
   - prolonged engagement criteria and role definition
   - notes about negative case analysis
   - process for selection of auditor, peer debriefer, and member checker

C. audit trail notes
   1. substance of trail
      - index to all records
   2. structure of trail
      - dates and cross-references on all records
   3. documentation strategy

5. notes about intentions and motivations

A. pre-inquiry proposal
   1. problem statements and methods
      - goals, objectives, and inquiry questions
      - intended methodology
      - relevant theoretical literature citations

B. personal notes
   1. reflexive notes
      - self-evaluation/criticism/limitations
   2. notes about motivations
      - theoretical preferences; prior investigation findings
   3. notes about expectations
      - methodological preferences
   4. (day-to-day) diary accounts

C. cognitive processes

6. instruments, tools and resources

A. guiding inquiry questions
   - observation formats
B. pilot/preliminary interview protocols
   - surveys
C. data collection tools
   - computer software
D. data analysis tools
   - bibliographies
   - list of contacts

files—contain the basic substantive information acquired during the evaluation; that is, information about the *phenomena* under investigation. These files contain information collected about the evaluand, context, setting, and so forth, and reflect how that information was reduced and then transformed into the findings and conclusions of the evaluation. *Process notes* include entries about the evaluator's behaviors and the methods employed. *Notes about intentions and motivations* contain personal information about the inquirer that he or she brought into the evaluation at its inception. The *instruments, tools, and resources files* contain all working documents that were used to standardize the data collection and analysis.

The second column (Forms of Data) describes in more detail the kinds of notes or records that could appear in the respective file types. They are intended to be comprehensive across all types of inquiries; we are not suggesting that every evaluation will include all of them. The forms of data illustrate the kinds of records and formats helpful for an audit.

The third column (Examples) contains a list of examples, and reflects the kinds of information that an auditor will be looking for when assessing trustworthiness or rigor. The next sections of this chapter explain the contents of Table 4.1.

AUDIT TRAIL FILES
REPRESENTING PHENOMENA
(ACTUAL EVENTS)

Raw data files, data reduction files, and data reconstruction files are all concerned with representing the actual phenomena (evaluand) under investigation. Each is explained below.

Raw Data Files

The closest the auditor gets to any evaluand is the raw data. Thus, the amount of faith the auditor places in the data will strongly influence the audit opinion. Raw data files comprise the universe of information from which findings are later derived. They include notes that provide information about events, conversations, and past histories. The types of raw data will depend on the individual evaluation and will vary with the purpose of the study and the data collection methods used.

```
Interview Respondent #12
Date: 6/3/86
```

	Interviewer:	So you like listening to music when you study.
1.	Respondent:	I always listen to music. I have to hear some noise.
	Interviewer:	Don't you find it distracting?
2.	Respondent:	No, I really don't pay attention to it. When there is music playing, or someone singing I really don't hear it. When someone is talking or when a commercial is on, I get distracted. So I usually put on an album.

Exhibit 4.1 Segment of an Interview Transcript

Raw data files consist of both filtered and unfiltered data. These data vary with the degree to which the evaluator interpreted the information before creating a written record. For example, the evaluator will normally filter what a respondent says or does when making interview or observational notes. In contrast, an audiotape recording represents a relatively unfiltered account of an interview in that the exact wording and language of the respondent comprises the raw data record. For our purposes, raw data (e.g., interview transcripts or interview writeups) will refer to all data prior to formal efforts to categorize or reduce them.

Raw data can also be characterized by the degree to which they are low on inference. We might say that the "rawest" data for each study will be low inference data. However, even these data are influenced by the evaluator's values, perspective, or interpretation that underlie the choice or construction of a low-inference measure.

By including times and dates on the raw data records, the auditee provides the auditor with evidence about the evolution of the study over time. Including a unique identifier on each datum (e.g. interview #1, #2) will provide a pointer to the particular interview respondent when the auditor tracks a finding to a source. When an evaluator extracts pieces of information from the raw data files during data reduction, marking the paragraphs or line numbers makes the auditor's tracking task much easier. This type of documentation will also help the evaluator when double checking his or her own entries at any time during the inquiry. An example of how these pointers work is shown in Exhibit 4.1.

In the example, the interview transcript is identified by #12 and the date (6/3/86). The sections of the transcript are numbered. (Each line could also have been numbered). The summary information that is extracted and placed in the data reduction file (e.g., onto a 3 × 5 card or in some other form) is circled. The circled section should then appear in the data reduction file with a note on it reflecting that it came from Interview #12, paragraph #2.

Unfiltered Accounts

Unfiltered raw data includes audiotapes (and transcripts), videotapes, and photographs. They are unfiltered insofar as they are not influenced by an interpretation. (One might argue that the videotape and photograph are filtered from the standpoint that they are framed, thereby intentionally excluding some information or emphasizing certain portions of the frame; Fang, 1986.) In cases in which the evaluator wants to rely on the precision of language, the auditor will likely place greater trust in unfiltered data such as an interview transcript (because it reflects the exact language of the respondent) than in filtered data such as nonverbatim writeups. Or, if visual information is critical to understanding the meanings of certain objects or symbols, again unfiltered records such as photographs will capture the information without suspicion that something was lost via a written description.

Filtered Accounts

Filtered raw data may be obtained unobtrusively, as in the case of records, documents, observational records and notes, or they may be obtained interactively, as in the case of interviews. Data are filtered insofar as the evaluator is taking notes about a subset of possible information being transmitted. For example, in the case of interviews, shorthand notes will include what is considered relevant at the time of the interview. Similarly, observational notes will focus on certain events while ignoring others. Notes about physical traces (Webb et al., 1966) will include descriptions about the physical setting under investigation, highlighting some things and not others. The evaluator should explain the strategy used when taking notes about events in order to instill confidence in the auditor that important information was not omitted from the raw data. Since the raw data will provide the base from which findings will be tracked, the auditor will seek assurance that the data accurately and completely reflect the evaluand and setting (i.e, the phenomena) under investigation.

Data Reduction Files

Data reduction files are created when the evaluator condenses the raw data to a form that is manageable. Miles and Huberman (1984,

---

Example of notes taken during an interview:

Our rewards are the satisfaction from doing the job well. They are
intangible rewards. We derive satisfaction from the students who profit
from the experience of taking these courses. People who don't value
student satisfaction are not going to have any incentives to do a good job
at teaching. Our department provides no tangible rewards; neither does
the university. Frankly, there is no payoff. I spend over 70% of my
working day directly or indirectly on teaching. In terms of tangible
rewards, I would be better cutting that down to 20-30%, but student
satisfaction is highly rewarding to me.

Example of condensed notes based on the interview:

Tangible rewards for excellent teaching are not given by the department or
the university.

The rewards are intrinsic and result from student satisfaction.

If student satisfaction were not rewarding, I would be better off reducing
the amount of time I spend on teaching.

Exhibit 4.2 Illustration of Data Reduction

p. 21) look at data reduction as "the process of selecting, focusing, simplifying, abstracting, and transforming the 'raw' data that appear in written-up field notes." These files are evidence of the evaluator's judgments about what to include and what to omit, a process of ranking the relative importance of the data. They should provide a shorter version of the information found in the raw data, one free from interpretation or criticism (Levine, 1985).

Some common forms of data reduction files include condensed summaries of observation or interview notes, lists of themes, or units of information. They often appear on 3×5 cards, on tally sheets, computer printouts, or even as highlighted sections of interview notes. As illustrated in the section on raw data, these abbreviated accounts should be linked with raw data through cross-references.

Condensed Notes

Condensed notes are further filtered accounts of the raw data. In condensed notes, items that the evaluator perceives as superfluous in the raw data will be eliminated. It is important that auditors be able to see how the condensed notes were derived from the raw data. Auditors will want assurance that they can rely on these notes as their own "raw data," because they are easier and faster to read than the evaluator's raw data. Exhibit 4.2 displays an excerpt from a set of interview notes (raw data) and a corresponding condensed note.

Writeups

Writeups are embellished versions of the raw data and are based on the evaluator's recall of what occurred. Miles and Huberman (1984, p. 50) suggest that the writeup "is a product intelligible to anyone" that can be read, coded, and analyzed. This is in contrast to field notes normally taken on-site, which are often in part illegible, contain abbreviations, and are sketchy.

Preparing the writeups should not be done solely for the auditor. It is usually done to ensure that the evaluator does not forget his or her own shorthand notes and details for elaboration. If we assume that details will be the most accurate if added very soon after the raw data are collected, the auditor is likely to look at write-ups with suspicion if they are completed days or weeks after data were collected.

Units of Information/Categories

In an effort to categorize raw data, an evaluator typically looks for recurrent units of information (Guba, 1978). Units are the "chunks" of information that are eventually combined to form categories that are, in turn, used to explain the evaluand under study. Units may be sentences, paragraphs or phrases capturing types of behavior, concerns or issues, definitions, concepts, or themes. Units are important because they are the building blocks that form categories, which, in turn, comprise the interpretive framework for the evaluation. Criteria for developing categories from units of information may include salience, frequency, uniqueness, interest, heuristic value, or importance (Bulmer, 1979; Guba, 1978; Guba & Lincoln, 1981). If we were to expand on the illustration presented in Exhibit 4.2 and examine additional examples of the condensed notes, we might find categories such as the following: perceptions about the university's concern for quality teaching, personal incentives for teaching, perceptions of reward structure, and so forth. In selecting units of information and developing categories, an evaluator (auditee) is advised to remember that the auditor will want to (1) track, via cross-references, how the categories were derived from the data, (2) understand the rationale for the choice of categories and the rules followed in sorting units into categories, and (3) follow the scheme used to code both units of information and categories.

Data Displays

Miles and Huberman (1984) illustrate a variety of data displays that they have found useful in their analyses. Displays refer to a "spatial format that presents information systematically to the user" (p. 79). Since the displays extract information from a wide cross-section of the data, they serve as summaries of large quantities of data. If matrices are used to display categories of data, the auditee should mark the rows and columns of the matrix with a code that cross-references the displayed data with the raw data and, if appropriate, with condensed notes. The auditor must be able to see how qualitative data were transformed into a tabular or display format.

Computer Analysis Summaries

Computers may be used to quantify survey results or to manage large amounts of interview data. When, for example, search and display software is used to identify instances of a particular word or phrase, the summary sheets available to the auditor should be explained. If the auditor is unfamiliar with the software, the evaluator should provide information on the sort, merge, and display algorithm used in the software package. Readers interested in learning more about the use of computers in qualitative data analysis might examine Conrad and Reinharz (1984) and Levine (1985).

Data Reconstruction Files

Data reconstruction files are created when the evaluator recombines the data from the data reduction files into a new set of categories or into a new picture or view of the investigation. Whereas the data *reduction* files may show what themes are important to interview #1, which are important to interview #2, and which are important to interview #N, the data *reconstruction* files will show which important themes are common to several interviews. Where the files for data reduction stop and where reconstruction begins is for all practical purposes arbitrary because they interact with each other continually during data collection and analysis. Thus, for example, data displays may appear in both types of files. Data reconstruction files illustrate the evaluator's efforts to group and regroup the data (categorize and recategorize the units), to draw inferences from the data, and to transform the data into a new perspective or interpretation.

Exhibit 4.3 displays an entry that an auditor might find in data reconstruction files. The example is from an organizational study in which the evaluator has identified four categories (A-D) with subcategories (Part A). The numbers appearing in parentheses are code

Personnel Problems (A)

lack of employee motivation (1,3,6,14)
people looking for new jobs (1,3,6,14,15)
few feel challenged (2,4,6,14,19)
unclear responsibilities (1-11,16-20)
low pay (1-20)

Power (C)

conflicts between leaders (2,4,5)
unbalanced department sizes (1-5,8,19)

Organizational Problems (B)

lack of agreed-upon goals (1,3,5,7,12)
small budget (1,3,5-20)
slow to change (1-20)
too large to manage (1,5,16-20)

Leadership Problems (D)

leadership ill-defined (2,3,5,12,13)
leaders don't like people (8,17)

Exhibit 4.3   Illustration of Data Reconstruction, Part A

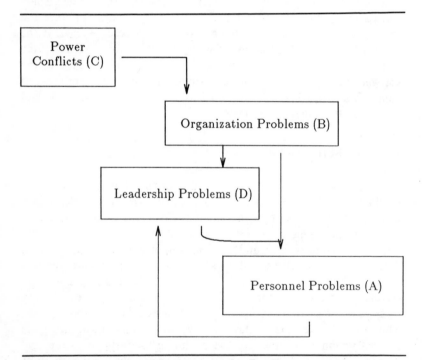

Exhibit 4.3   Illustration of Data Reconstruction, Part B

numbers for various interview respondents. These code numbers allow
the auditor to track the development of categories and subcategories
back to the raw and reduced data.

In establishing relationships between categories, the evaluator in this study may have hypothesized that organizational problems (B)—lack of agreement on goals and small budget—have led to lack of employee motivation and unclear responsibilities (personnel problems, A). He or she might also have speculated that conflicts between leaders have created confusion about direction and goals, which, in turn, has made it difficult for leaders to manage and for employees to do their jobs. If this were the reasoning of the evaluator in this study, the auditor might expect to find a display in the evaluator's notes that looked like Exhibit 4.3 (Part B). The auditor will also expect to find a dated description of rationale for this developing interpretation in the data reconstruction files.

This exhibit illustrates a very simple case of what an auditor might see as an evolving structure of evaluation findings. The auditor should be able to trace this (and refined versions of this) structure to the categories of data and, from the categories, work backwards to the actual interviews (or field notes) where the data originated.

Findings from which conclusions will be drawn originate in this process of data reconstruction. Findings are statements about the evaluand that the evaluator has evidence to believe are credible and supported by the data. Conclusions are judgments about the findings that the evaluator wishes to emphasize in the final evaluation report. Four types of data reconstruction files are discussed below.

Theoretical Notes

Theoretical notes are derived by categorizing field notes and reactions. New ideas are often triggered when writing up field notes and serve as working hypotheses. The categories of information form the structure of the emerging findings. The evaluator's notes should show the efforts to group and regroup the data in order to create a category structure or descriptive story. They will range from notes about hunches and speculations early in the study to drafts of findings and conclusions derived later in the study.

New theoretical relationships and perspectives should continue to evolve during the study until theoretical saturation is reached (Glaser & Strauss, 1967; Glaser, 1978). Saturation refers to the phenomenon in which no new data are discovered to help the evaluator generate new categories or further develop existing categories (Glaser & Strauss, 1967). The relationship between existing data and new data can be highlighted for auditor review by describing how the new data add more evidence to the emerging interpretation (redundancy), or suggest that the interpretation be changed to accommodate them (revision).

Relationships Among Categories

The evaluator's files should contain displays that show the relationships between and among categories. They illustrate the theoretical or interpretive framework being built. This framework will, in turn, be used by the evaluator in describing the phenomena under study.

Categories should be defined, using examples from the raw data. The categories should also be explained relative to other categories, and relative to evaluation findings in other similar evaluation contexts (if appropriate). Establishing relationships between categories has

> the prime function of integrating the theory [interpretation or perspective] and rendering [it] dense and saturated as the relationships increase. These functions then lead to theoretical completeness accounting for as much variation in a pattern of behavior with as few concepts as possible, thereby, maximizing parsimony and scope. (Glaser, 1978, p. 93)

Findings and Conclusions

In the files containing findings and conclusions, the auditor must be able to recognize the overall perspective or interpretation being offered, and how it relates to the categories of data. If the interpretation is not logical and internally homogeneous, the activity of tracing the category examples or the category labels back to the raw data has little meaning. The auditor could attest to the fact that statements of findings can be traced to the raw data, but that they were not meaningfully interrelated nor do they help the reader of the evaluation report understand the overall evaluation results. Conclusions are the evaluator's interpretations of the findings, and they should be cross-referenced with appropriate findings to show the relationships.

When findings and conclusions contain generalized statements that use words such as *all, many, several,* or *most,* the auditor will verify the accuracy of those modifiers. As Miles and Huberman (1984, p. 231) state, "from one or two concrete, vivid instances, we assume there are dozens more lurking in the bushes—but we don't verify whether or how many there are, and there are usually fewer than we think."

Reports

Reports may be written on an interim basis or when the inquiry is complete. In examining the various drafts of reports (including any notes prepared for oral reports), the auditor will be attempting to verify the fact that the evaluator's perspective or predispositions did not shape the inquiry too heavily, and that the evaluator was open to new information and acted in a responsive fashion. The auditor will (1) determine whether (and why) the evaluator retracted or modified an important conclusion; (2) examine the extent to which ongoing methodological decisions and changing category schemes are reflected in reports, and (3) investigate whether or not the evaluator conveniently fit data into a structure or interpretation that the evaluator had in mind prior to conducting the evaluation.

AUDIT TRAIL FILES
REPRESENTING INQUIRY PROCEDURES

In addition to the files of notes that represent the phenomena or events under study, there is a second set of files representing the inquiry or evaluation procedures. These files contain (1) notes about the evaluation process, (2) notes about intentions and motivations, and (3) copies of instruments, tools, and resources.

Process Notes

Process notes explain the procedures used, decisions made, and rationale for the entire evaluation. These notes represent the information most likely to help the auditor understand the lines of thinking during the inquiry and least likely to appear in a public report. Process notes should illustrate what the evaluator did, why, and with what effect. Three types of process notes include methodological notes, notes about trustworthiness and audit trail notes.

Methodological Notes

Methodological notes include information about procedures, strategies, and day-to-day decisions throughout the study. Each type of information is briefly described below.

Procedures. A running account of all procedures, strategies, and rationale should be described in the audit trail. The evaluator should log the essential field behaviors such as tactics chosen and sampling decisions. The evaluator may choose to maintain these accounts as separate journal entries or integrate them with the raw data. In these methodological notes, the evaluator should document and describe each methodological decision (e.g., who was interviewed, what document was used, what was observed, how and when data were summarized and analyzed, etc.) and provide a rationale (e.g., decision was based on initial evaluation plan, decision emerged from a working hypothesis). In sum, notes about procedures should describe what was done, and when, thereby providing a detailed diary of every evaluator activity during the study.

Strategies. Strategy notes should explain some of the higher level decisions as opposed to the daily decisions. For example, they should describe the procedures used to analyze the data, the criteria used to gauge theoretical importance, theoretical saturation, and the guidelines used to ascertain how many more respondents to interview. They should explain the planning of the evaluation, how it was determined what methods to use and why methods may have been altered.

Decisions and rationale. Because the design of a naturalistic evaluation emerges, each evaluator decision should be responsive to some other tactic or some new data. The evaluator should document why he or she chose the next interviewee, how he or she chose a data analytic technique, what criteria were used to bound the inquiry, and why he or she is confident that theoretical saturation has been attained. Each of these decisions should be cross-referenced within the context of the study. For example, if during an interview, a respondent lacked some information, the respondent may have suggested someone whom the interviewer might contact to obtain that information. This lead should be noted in the methodological notes and cross-referenced in the appropriate interviews.

A record of ongoing decisions is of utmost importance to the auditor. This record illustrates the mind-set of the evaluator, providing reasons for decisions. It is through these notes that the auditor will be able to ascertain whether or not the day-to-day inquiry decisions were sound and reasonable. In addition, a review of the methodological notes will allow the auditor to verify whether the methodological descriptions in the final report are accurate in view of the audit trail accounts. The first judgment is made about the integrity of the ongoing decisions. The second judgment is an attestation that the descriptions in the methods section of the final report are accurate, given the methodological notes.

Notes About Trustworthiness

Information about efforts to enhance trustworthiness (Guba, 1981; Lincoln & Guba, 1985) should appear in the audit trail. Trustworthiness notes document the effort to ensure credibility, confirmability, and dependability as defined earlier. (These criteria will be discussed more fully in Chapter 5) The trustworthiness notes should describe how and when methods were used to achieve these criteria, and with what effect.

At one level, notes about trustworthiness will allow the auditor to verify that there is evidence in the audit trail supporting the methods described in the report. At a deeper level, by reading about the accounts of member checking, efforts to triangulate, and so forth, the auditor can determine whether these activities were appropriately integrated into the methods and whether the outcomes of the particular activities were folded back into the design of methods.

Credibility notes. Credibility notes will contain descriptions of efforts to ensure credibility, what the results of these efforts were, and how they contributed to the evaluation. For example, if the evaluator debriefed with peers, notes about those meetings should be generated. If debriefing changed the direction of the inquiry, it should be explained. Similarly, the evaluator may keep notes on member-check activities, describing how and when the member checks were implemented. Lincoln & Guba (1985) provide a detailed procedure for member checks, which includes: (1) selecting a review panel; (2) preparing and delivering the information packet; (3) holding the review meeting; and (4) considering inputs from the member check process. The audit trail notes on credibility should describe this member check procedure as it unfolds. For example, the notes should describe how the panel was selected and who comprised it, what information was included in the packet, how and why it was selected, and the procedures followed during the review meeting.

The notes should describe whether information presented by the evaluator has been verified or disputed by the stakeholders. If the information is not agreed upon by all parties, the evaluator should explain in the audit trail credibility notes what was changed in order to reach agreement. Finally, the evaluator should document why the disagreement occurred, and whether it could have been prevented. The auditor will be interested to learn whether a stakeholder had a problem because the finding lacked truth value, or because he or she did not like the finding. If the finding lacked truth value, the auditor will be alerted to potential unwanted evaluator bias or to possible shortcomings in the evaluation methodology. If the finding was unpopular, the auditor would focus on how the evaluator accommodated this stakeholder concern without sacrificing the integrity of the findings.

Credibility notes should also contain information about triangulation procedures, illustrating, for example, the interplay between combining multiple data collection techniques (e.g., interviews, observations, questionnaires) and how the application of each technique influenced results of the other techniques. In particular, if the results from different techniques varied, the evaluator should describe what was done to resolve the divergence, and how the findings ultimately reflect that fact.

Dependability notes. Dependability notes describe how the evaluator designed and implemented the study in a way that promoted dependability. The very act of assembling an audit trail to meet the requirements spelled out in this chapter can enhance dependability. The evaluator is advised to document other procedures used to enhance dependability and to control unwanted bias (e.g., describing efforts to prevent cooptation, describing how day-to-day decisions related to following important leads).

Confirmability notes. Since confirmability assessments focus on neutrality of the findings, confirmability notes should contain explanations of how the evaluator ensured that the findings of the study are grounded in the data, are logical, and are useful. These notes should describe how the auditee designed an audit trail to enable an outside auditor to attest to confirmability, and how he or she tried to verify his or her own findings.

Audit Trail Notes

The auditee is advised to explain the organization of the documentation by clearly labeling the audit trail files. An auditee's notes about the structure of the audit trail items will be extremely helpful for the auditor in examining the linkages between audit trail entries. By compiling a table or index of audit trail contents, the auditee helps the auditor to see at a glance how the audit trail is structured. This index will also serve as a road map into the audit trail.

Notes About Intentions and Motivations

Notes about intentions and motivations reveal evaluator predispositions at the inception of the inquiry and feelings and attitudes during the inquiry. These notes should contain information illustrating the personal biases of the evaluator and how he or she ensured that these biases were sufficiently controlled so as not to influence the evaluation findings. Three sources of information about intentions and motivations may be found in the audit trail including, the preinquiry proposal, personal notes, and notes about cognitive processes.

Preinquiry Proposal

Potential evaluator biases and preferences brought into the study can be seen in part in an evaluation proposal that describes the relevant literature, the proposed design and methodology, and the evaluator's background and credentials. The auditor should examine the proposal in combination with methodological notes to ensure that the evaluator was responsive during the inquiry as opposed to being driven solely by the framework described in the proposal.

Personal Notes

Personal notes include accounts of the feelings experienced by the evaluator. Entries should be made about decisions, procedures, activities, introspections, fears, and biases, as well as values and interests (Lincoln & Guba, 1985). The evaluator keeps personal notes for catharsis and to monitor his or her own changing values during the study. For the auditor, personal notes provide an opportunity to see how evaluator fears are addressed. It also allows the auditor to determine whether the evaluator's values change, and if so, whether this is a result of cooptation or other political influences.

It is important for the evaluator to describe his or her personal interests in the evaluand under investigation. To accomplish this, Covert (personal communication) suggests that the evaluator prepare a statement prior to the start of the study in which he or she describes his or her expectations for the study. This will help the auditor determine the degree to which the evaluator's expectations and personal interests may have guided the inquiry and influenced conclusions in spite of data and findings to the contrary. In a naturalistic evaluation, the evaluator should be open to new interpretive frameworks, and although the auditor might expect to find an existing body of knowledge or point of view as a starting point, he or she will be concerned if it is perceived as a predetermined conclusion.

Cognitive Processes

It is extremely difficult to understand the evaluator's mental processes employed in focusing the evaluation. What the evaluator comes to understand, and what he or she chooses to represent in the final report is the result of complex cognitive processes that guide decisions about how to represent the phenomena both internally (to themselves as inquirer) and externally (to a readership). Throughout the evaluation, the inquirer will continually make assumptions, judge sources of information, filter and prioritize information, and make inferences from the data. Although an auditor would not expect the evaluator to keep separate files describing these cognitive processes, he or she might expect to see some description of the thought processes used in deciding what information makes its way into the notes and how that information is used.

Instruments, Tools, and Resources

The audit trail should contain copies of tools and instruments used to guide data collection and analysis. These will principally include interview protocols, observation formats, questionnaires, and a description of computer software. Since the tools may be revised during the evaluation, the dates of different versions should be noted. These tools and resources should also be cross-referenced with the process note entries that describe why they were used, how they were developed, and why they were changed.

Guiding Questions

At the beginning of an evaluation, an initial set of questions will guide the inquiry and direct methodological decisions. The set of questions will grow and evolve and shape decisions about data collection procedures as the evaluation unfolds.

Pilot/Preliminary Interview Protocols

The preliminary interview protocol is the list of questions or question areas that the evaluator used at the beginning of the inquiry. They reflect the preconceived notions the evaluator might have about the evaluand and the setting under investigation, and serve as a starting point for the first interview.

Data Collection Tools

These tools will include survey instruments, as well as modifications to the lists of guiding questions and interview protocol questions. If observations are conducted, this might include any instrument that was used to help standardize observational data.

Data Analysis Tools

Data analysis tools will include formats for manual data displays or any computer software. If computer software is used, records should include the name of the software and the function it performed. If it is used for sorting or tallying, the auditee should explain the sorting rules in the software design and the way in which the display capabilities influenced data collection, data entry, and data analysis. Limitations of the software capabilities should also be acknowledged.

SUMMARY

This chapter has presented a view of the procedures that an evaluator might follow to develop an audit trail of a naturalistic evaluation, and it has suggested several kinds of files that an auditor would find useful during an audit. Preparing an audit trail is important in cases in which the evaluator would like an impartial, external auditor to evaluate the inquiry design, to confirm that the findings were logically derived, and that the day-to-day decisions were in accord with generally accepted inquiry practices. By developing the various types of files, and by cross-referencing audit trail entries across files, the auditee will make it possible for an independent auditor to cross-check the entries and grasp the gestalt of the inquiry expediently. The audit trail is also a tool that an evaluator can use to monitor the quality of an evaluation as it unfolds. The very activity of maintaining an audit trail encourages reflexivity and a careful review of procedure.

The auditor will examine the *substance* of the audit trail (raw data, data reduction notes, and data reconstruction notes, methodological notes) to "replay" the inquiry. When, for example, the auditor reads about a methodological choice (e.g., who to interview), he or she will attempt to: (1) verify what the auditee discovered (raw data records), (2) learn how the auditee conducted the interview (methodological notes), and (3) understand how the auditee evaluated the interview (personal notes). When the auditor reads about an analytic strategy (methodological notes) and the resulting categories (reconstructed data), he or she will attempt to compare it to discrete items in the data (raw data; reduction notes). Documentation of the data analytic strategies will show the auditor how the evaluator reduced interview data into a manageable product. The auditor will be interested in the processes that guided the analysis and any instruments used to aid the analysis. This documentation is important because it will help the auditor assess whether the inquirer selected an appropriate technique and whether he or she properly implemented that technique.

When the dates of each entry are recorded in the audit trail, the auditor will be able to recreate the actual sequence of evaluator behaviors and thought processes and to cross-check audit trail items. When the audit trail is not extensive and is missing proper cross-references, it may still be possible to conduct an audit. However, it will likely take much more time, will require the evaluator to answer more questions during the audit, and may not stimulate the same level of confidence in the inquiry being audited.

EXERCISES

1. Imagine that you are planning an evaluation. Describe the types of records you would keep in anticipation of being audited. Describe some ways in which preparing for an audit would be advantageous for you during the inquiry. Describe some ways in which you think it would be disadvantageous.

2. Explain how the construction of an audit trail both enhances auditability and contributes to the reliability and dependability of an evaluation.

3. Why is it important to keep files both illustrating the evaluator's behaviors and explaining data gathering, analysis, and interpretation?

4. One of the authors recently conducted an evaluation of a business training program designed to increase the general business awareness of junior staff and to improve communications and cooperation of staff across divisions. A total of 20 individuals, including program developers, program administrators, program facilitators, office management, and managers supervising staff involved in the

program were interviewed as representatives of various stakeholding groups. Some of these interviews were conducted in person, some by telephone, and several individuals were interviewed more than once. Four group discussions/ debriefings were held with participants in the program. Data were also gathered from all participants via a short questionnaire containing both forced-choice and open-ended items. In addition, approximately 250 pages of documents pertaining to program history, operations, objectives, administration, and cost were examined. Several sessions of the training program were also observed. Sketch a system of internal control for managing the data that were collected and subsequently analyzed.

5. Imagine that you are the auditor who is examining the evaluation referred to in Exercise 4 and that you are looking for evidence of the integrity and dependability of evaluation procedures. What kind of audit trail files would you expect to see? What would those files contain?

6. Review the section on Personal Notes in this chapter, then prepare a statement about yourself in which you describe your characteristics as a human instrument.

5

Auditing an Inquiry

This chapter discusses a detailed application of the general audit model described in Chapter 2. It is addressed to the prospective auditor who plans to audit a naturalistic evaluation against criteria established for trustworthiness or rigor (Guba & Lincoln, 1981; Lincoln & Guba, 1985). However, it also explains what the evaluator (auditee) must do during the initial stages of an audit to elicit the aid of an auditor and to arrange the logistics of the audit. In addition, a list of open-ended questions for focusing the audit is presented. Focusing questions are used rather than requirements because evaluation auditing practices are not yet sufficiently mature to have stringent audit requirements. The general audit procedure is divided into five stages, including:

(1) preparing for an audit,
(2) assessing auditability and negotiating the contract,
(3) formalizing the contract,
(4) preparing and implementing a work program to determine trustworthiness, and
(5) preparing the audit report.

Emphasis will be placed on the fourth stage—determining trustworthiness—because this is the major purpose of the audit. The first three stages discuss some of the logistical considerations and the issues relevant to negotiation and committing to the audit process. The last stage briefly covers the development of an audit report.

Table 5.1 displays the five-stage audit procedure. The first column (Events) shows the five stages comprising 11 separate events or milestones of the audit. The second column (Auditee Tasks) describes the auditee's role prior to and during audit negotiations. The third column (Auditor Tasks) contains a list of tasks the auditor must complete as part of his or her role. The tasks are associated with each event from column 1. When both the auditor and auditee are jointly involved in an event, this is noted by a box spanning the columns labeled "Auditee Tasks" and "Auditor Tasks." The fourth column (Focusing Questions/Issues for the Auditor & Referent Audit File Types) serves to guide and focus the audit. The questions listed in this column should be viewed as prompts for the auditor, suggesting areas within the audit trail worth investigating. The relative importance of the "yes" and "no" responses to the focusing questions must be determined by the auditor; we have made no attempt to establish weights or priorities.

Accompanying each focusing question in parentheses are series of numbers referring to the files presented in the previous chapter. These references indicate where within the audit trail (i.e., which file types and forms of data) an auditor must look in order to address each question. To address most of the focusing questions, it will be necessary to look in combinations of files and to cross-check and compare them. When looking through Table 5.1, the reader may notice that most of the confirmability questions (see Event D.7) can be addressed by looking at the three types of data files (raw data, data reduction, and data reconstruction files). In combination, these will show how data were transformed into the conclusions. In contrast, most of the dependability questions (Event D.8) are addressed by cross-checking the process notes and notes about intentions and motivations.

The remainder of this chapter describes the auditing procedure event by event. It explains what tasks the auditor must complete, and what he or she looks for during an audit.

PREPARING FOR AN AUDIT

In the early stages of preparing for the audit (Events A.1-A.3), the auditee (evaluator) assumes the proactive role. He or she determines whether or not to contract with an outside auditor, and whether or not to initiate the contact. Each event within this stage is described below.

Evaluator Requests Audit

Preparation for the audit begins with the auditee's efforts to contact an auditor. The auditee will likely look for colleagues with method-

(text continues on page 115)

TABLE 5.1

Procedure for Auditing Naturalistic Evaluations

Events	Auditee Tasks	Auditor Tasks	Focusing Questions/Issues for Auditor (and Referent Audit Trail Files)
A. Preparing for an Audit			
1. evaluator requests audit	A. determine need for audit B. prepare audit trail for review C. initiate contact		
2. orientation to the evaluation	A. explain record-keeping system	A. become familiar with organization of audit trail B. become familiar with the evaluand	(4C) (1A/3D/5A)
3. discuss alternatives	A. discuss proposed audit scope and standards		
	auditor and auditee decide jointly to continue with audit unconditionally, conditionally, with a new auditor, or abandon audit		
B. Assessing Auditability and Negotiating the Contract			
4. become familiar with study		A. identify evaluation questions & problems B. identify methodological choices 1. paradigm	(3D/5A) (3D/4A/5A)

5. determine auditability

A. arrange logistics for auditor
B. remain available for consultation

2. techniques
C. identify major substantive issues
D. identify findings and conclusions

A. become familiar with audit trail
   1. review audit trail files (substance)
   2. review audit trail structure
   3. become familiar with coding scheme
   4. identify linkages between and within audit trail files
   5. determine how characteristics of the audit trail will affect the audit

(3D/5A)
(3B, C)

How complete is the audit trail?
Do the following exist?
   1. raw data (1)
   2. data reduction files (2)
   3. data reconstruction files (3)
   4. process notes (4)
   5. notes on intentions and motivations (5)
   6. instruments, tools, resources (6)

How comprehensible is the audit trail?
   1. Does the derivation of each audit trail component make sense? (4A, C)
   2. Is the structure of the audit trail self-explanatory? (4A, C)

How useful is the audit trail?
   1. Do materials contain dates? (1-6)
   2. Are all materials cross-referenced? (1-6)
   3. Are all materials indexed? (4C)
   4. Are there explanations about the purpose of each audit trail file? (4C)

(continued)

TABLE 5.1 Continued

Events	Auditee Tasks	Auditor Tasks	Focusing Questions/Issues for Auditor (and Referent Audit Trail Files)
B. Assessing Auditability and Negotiating the Contract (cont.)		B. determine how the nature of the evaluation will affect the audit C. determine how available time will affect the audit D. determine whether early involvement of the auditor will affect the audit E. determine how the auditor's background characteristics affect the audit	1. Do the auditor's background characteristics complement the evaluation?
	C. review auditor's characteristics & qualifications		
	auditor and auditee jointly discuss audit scope, objectives, and standards		
	A. revise audit trail as necessary B. discuss logistics to proceed	A. make recommendations as necessary B. discuss logistics C. determine boundaries of the audit	
	auditor and auditee jointly decide whether to contract for the audit		
C. Formalizing the Contract			
6. negotiate contract			

D. Preparing and Implementing an Audit Work Program to Determine Trustworthiness

7. assess confirmability

   a. assess whether findings are grounded in the data

      A. sample findings
      B. identify audit trail files linked to each finding
      C. verify that the linkage exists
      D. assess incidence of undisciplined subjectivity

      1. Can all findings be mapped to data reduction files and to raw data? (1/2A/3C)
      2. Does relative weighting given to categories reflect their prevalence in the data? (1/2A/3/4A/6D)
      3. Is there imposition of evaluator's terminology in data? (1B/2A/3C/5A, B/6A)
      4. Is there sufficient description of evaluator's tacit filtering processes? (1B/4A, B/5B, C)

   b. assess whether inferences are logical

      A. identify analytic strategies
      B. assess application of strategies
      C. assess accuracy of the descriptions of the phenomena and concepts

      1. Has appropriate analytic technique been selected? (4A/5A/6D)
      2. Has the analytic technique been applied properly? (2A/3A, B/6D)

(continued)

TABLE 5.1 Continued

Events	Auditee Tasks	Auditor Tasks	Focusing Questions/Issues for Auditor (and Referent Audit Trail Files)
D. Preparing and Implementing an Audit Work Program to Determine Trustworthiness (cont.)			
	b. assess whether inferences are logical (cont.)	D. determine whether inferences are unsubstantiated or illogical	3. Are units of analysis compatible with data? (1/2A/3B)
			4. Do category labels accurately describe the concepts? (2A/3B)
			5. Do examples clearly explain categories? Do category labels reflect examples? (2A/3A, B, C)
			6. Do examples fairly represent data? (1/3A, B, C)
			7. Do categories reflect emerging working hypotheses? (2A/3A, B)
			8. Are alternative inferences (alternative explanations) possible? (1/2A/3A/4A/5B/6C/D)
			9. Are there unexplained phenomena (unused data)? (1/2A/3B, C)
	c. assess utility of category structure	A. examine clarity of category/conceptual structure	1. Is there evidence of category overlap? (2A/3B, D)
		B. assess explanatory power of structure	2. Is there an unintended mixture of levels of analysis? (1/2A/3B)
		C. assess fit between categories, definitions, and examples	3. Has an optimal set of categories been extracted? (1/2A/3B2/4A/5C)
			4. Are categories exhaustive of the data? Do they support saturation?

d. assess whether the evaluator accounted for discrepant data

    (2A/3A, B/4A/6D)

    5. Are categories mutually exclusive? (2A/3B, C)

    6. Do categories describe phenomena at same level of detail? (1/2A/3B)

A. assess the design and implementation of confirmability efforts

    1. Are there sufficient efforts to ensure confirmability? (4A, B)

    2. Does evaluator account for/accommodate negative evidence? (3A, D/4A/5B)

8. assess dependability

    a. assess appropriateness of inquiry decisions and methodological shifts

        A. identify inquiry decisions and rationale

        B. identify working hypotheses

        1. Is there a clear relationship between working hypotheses and sampling decisions? (3A/4A)

        2. Is there evidence of systematic process for changing the instrumentation? (3A/4A)

        3. Is there support for altering techniques? (3A/4A/5B)

    b. assess degree and incidence of evaluator bias

        A. identify decisions and rationale to bound the evaluation

        1. Is there evidence of early closure? (3A/4A3/5B)

        2. Are there unitized, uncategorized data? (2A3, 4/3B)

        3. Is there evidence disproving claim of saturation? (3A, B/4A)

(continued)

TABLE 5.1 Continued

Events	Auditee Tasks	Auditor Tasks	Focusing Questions/Issues for Auditor (and Referent Audit Trail Files)
D. Preparing and Implementing an Audit Work Program to Determine Trustworthiness (cont.)			
b. assess degree and incidence of evaluator bias (cont.)	A. identify decisions and rationale to bound the evaluation (cont.)		4. Are there unexplored areas which appear in the field notes? (1/2A/3A/4A3/5A)
			5. Is there unnecessarily strict adherence to interview schedule? (4A/5A/6)
			6. Was the study discontinued to meet a deadline? (5A, B)
			7. Was focus influenced by sponsoring agency? (5A, B)
			8. Is there sufficient search for negative cases? (3A/4A)
	B. identify instances which may suggest cooptation		1. Is there identification with authority figure(s) in the setting? (4A/5B)
			2. Are there shifts in feelings of empathy? (3A/4A/5B)
			3. Is there unused, conflicting evidence? (2A/3C/4B/5C)
			4. Is there unexplained neglect of potential leads? (3A/4A/5A, B)
	C. identify whether ungrounded judgments are made		1. Is there overemphasis on personal notes in analysis? (2A2/5B/6D)
			2. Is there sufficient support to substantiate methodological choices? (3A/4A)

D. assess whether there is a Pygmalion effect

1. Is there unfounded convergence of personal and field notes? (2A/5B/6D)
2. Do the field notes reflect proposal too closely? (1/2A/5A)

E. assess whether there is a Hawthorne effect

1. Do outcome categories reflect preliminary questions too closely? (3B, C/6A, B)
2. Is there unexplained similarity in language between respondents and evaluator's initial position? (2A/5A/6A)

F. identify evidence of triangulation

1. Is there unbalanced reliance on one method? (4A, 3B/5A/6C)
2. Is there relationship between working hypotheses and selection of information sources? (3A/4A)

9. review credibility

a. review the design and implementation of credibility strategies

A. look for evidence of strategies used to enhance credibility

1. Is there evidence of triangulation? (3C/4A, B)
2. Is there evidence of member checking? (3C/4B)
3. Is there evidence of preliminary validations (ongoing member checks)? (4A, B)
4. Is there evidence of peer debriefing? (4A/B)

(continued)

113

TABLE 5.1 Continued

Events	Auditee Tasks	Auditor Tasks	Focusing Questions/Issues for Auditor (and Referent Audit Trail Files)
D. Preparing and Implementing an Audit Work Program to Determine Trustworthiness (cont.)			
a. review the design and implementation of credibility strategies (cont.)		A. look for evidence of strategies used to enhance credibility (cont.)	5. Are the raw data isomorphic with phenomena under investigation? (1/2A) 6. Is there evidence of negative case analysis? (3A/4B) 7. Are referential adequacy materials available? (1A/4B) 8. Is there evidence of prolonged engagement?
b. review the impact of credibility strategies on methodological choices, data sources, and findings			1. Is there evidence of responsive flexibility? (3A/4A/5A, B)
E. Preparing the Audit Report			
10. feedback and renegotiation	A. assess accuracy of auditor claims B. assess adherence/fulfillment to contract/agreement	A. present findings B. discuss discrepancies and determine nature of closure	
11. complete agreement		A. write final report	

ological expertise to conduct the audit or contact members of the professional society of evaluators (the American Evaluation Association) for possible candidates. As noted in the previous chapter, it is most advantageous for the auditor if the auditee has prepared the evaluation with an audit in mind. This will increase the likelihood that the appropriate documentation will be maintained. If an audit trail was not prepared during the evaluation, the auditee is advised to assemble and organize all documentation before beginning the search for an auditor.

Orientation to the Evaluation

During the first meeting of auditor and auditee, the auditee will describe the study to the prospective auditor, explain his or her record-keeping system, and discuss initial thoughts about the audit scope and standards. The evaluator is advised to describe the types of files kept, the ways they are cross-referenced, the size of the study, the nature of the evaluand under investigation, and the time frame for the audit. This initial contact might be completed on the telephone, by mail, or in person.

At this early stage, the auditor seeks to become sufficiently familiar with the proposed audit scope and the general organization of the audit trail to decide whether or not he or she is interested in or capable of conducting the audit. These steps in an evaluation audit (with the possible exception of program audits conducted by the GAO) differ from a financial audit in which the audit may be mandated and for which there is a sizable talent pool from which to draw upon auditing services.

Discuss Alternatives

As a result of the initial contact, the auditor and auditee should reach a preliminary agreement to proceed with planning for the audit. The auditee may make some changes in the audit trail at this point as part of the agreement. These changes might include reordering the files, providing a better index, adding some cross-references, and so forth. Alternatively, the auditee may decide not to be audited, or may prefer to shop around for a different auditor.

ASSESSING AUDITABILITY AND
NEGOTIATING THE CONTRACT

As discussed in Chapter 2, the second stage of the audit requires making a preliminary auditability assessment and setting the audit scope and objectives. An audit is dependent on the composition and structure of the audit trail because the audit trail provides source material that does not appear in a written final report. The certainty and efficiency with which auditor conclusions are drawn is directly attributable to the completeness and comprehensibility of the audit trail. In this stage of the procedure, the auditor assesses whether the study is auditable, clarifies the audit scope and standards to be applied, and eventually reaches a formal agreement with the auditee.

Become Familiar with the Study

Once the auditor and auditee agree to continue, the auditor will inquire about the study in greater depth. The auditor will discuss with the auditee those issues that are relevant to the investigation of the evaluand (e.g., setting, context), the nature of findings and conclusions, and issues relevant to the selection of an inquiry paradigm and methods. It is important for the auditor to be knowledgeable about inquiry methods as well as about substantive issues in order to conduct an informed audit examination. If the auditor does not have the necessary level of expertise in methods and lacks familiarity with substantive issues, the evaluation may need to be audited by a different auditor.

Determine Auditability

The auditability assessment really begins with the auditor's first impression of the audit trail structure and general organization. Since first impressions can be misleading, he or she is advised to review the audit trail closely before committing to conduct the audit. The auditee facilitates this review by arranging logistics for auditor access to the trail and by remaining available to answer questions. Additional auditor tasks in this stage include determining how factors unique to the evaluation may affect the audit, how the time available to conduct the audit may constrain scope, and how auditor characteristics and qualifications affect the decision to audit. At the close of this stage, auditor and auditee discuss audit scope and objectives and decide whether to enter into a formal agreement for conducting the audit examination.

Become Familiar with the Audit Trail

A careful assessment of the completeness, comprehensiveness, and interrelationships of audit trail components cannot be overemphasized. The audit trail is the auditor's primary source of evidence for tracking auditee performance and for attesting to auditee claims. It is the record of the evaluation process and provides the rationale for the auditee's methodological decisions as well as the evidence demonstrating how interpretations and findings appearing in the final evaluation report were grounded in the data. Therefore, before entering into a contract or signing a letter of agreement with the auditee, the auditor must attempt to identify both the strengths and potential shortcomings of the audit trail.

An auditability assessment is a risk assessment. By becoming acquainted with the audit trail, the auditor is attempting to identify possible control risk attributable to the auditee's record-keeping system. He or she also is attempting to form a view of potential inherent risks in the auditee's data-gathering and analysis procedures. Of course, it is possible that shortcomings in the trail of evidence may become apparent only after the audit is underway. An auditor may find that the audit examination is impeded by incomplete cross-references, gaps in methodological notes, missing data, and so forth. By conducting a thorough review of the auditee's records before beginning an examination, the auditor is attempting to minimize this risk as well.

In general, becoming familiar with the audit trail involves reviewing the overall design of the documentation system, particularly whether the files are neat, distinguishable from one another, and have multiple cross-references and dates. The auditor should assess the usefulness of the index as a road map for locating components of the audit trail. He or she should determine the ease with which the various audit trail components can be identified and linked together through cross-references and dates provided in the files. The audit trail should be self-contained, and with minimal discussion, self explanatory. The linkages that connect various representations of the data (raw data, data reduction, data synthesis) should be obvious as should linkages between the representations of data and the methodological choices (e.g., theoretical/purposive sampling).

The attributes of the audit trail most likely to affect the audit are its substance, structure, and volume. The *substance* refers to the actual files that are kept, including: (1) raw data files; (2) data reduction files; (3) data reconstruction files; (4) process notes; (5) notes about intentions and motivations; and (6) instruments, tools, and resources.

The following examples illustrate the importance of these files from the auditor's perspective: If it is not apparent how process notes and data reduction files explain data reduction, it will be difficult or impossible for the auditor to assess the evaluator's view of what was important in the data and what was excluded; insufficient methodological notes will clearly impair or prevent the auditor from understanding the logic behind methodological decisions. Without an accurate record of these decisions, the auditor will not be able to offer an informed opinion on the integrity of the methodology. Comprehensive records showing data, reduction files, and reconstruction notes in combination with process notes will enable the auditor to assess confirmability, particularly whether findings are grounded in the data, and whether the inferences are logical. In sum, the ability of the auditor to make certain types of audit judgments depends on the files available for scrutiny.

The *structure* of the audit trail refers to the cross-references, index, and dates in the files. What the auditor can do in a given period of time will be influenced by the tracking mechanism supplied by the evaluator. Dates will allow the auditor to reconstruct sequences. The cross-references will allow faster tracking. If the cross-references are incomplete, the auditor will have to look through much more information to track findings to raw data, and to track the relationship between theoretical notes and methodological notes. The absence of these features may make the task so laborious that the auditor may decide not to conduct the audit. Or, the absence of these features may require the auditor to spend so much more time that the cost of the audit may be prohibitive.

Volume refers simply to the amount of material at the auditor's disposal. This can be measured in number of pages of raw data or number of pages of the audit trail. Clearly the volume will affect sampling decisions by the auditor and the percentage of items the auditor will be able to track in a given period of time. Volume could also indicate complexity, thereby influencing time required for the auditor to become sufficiently familiar with the evaluand and the findings of the evaluation.

Determine How the
Nature of the Evaluation
Will Affect the Audit

A study's size, its methodology, the object of the evaluation and the goals of the evaluation will affect audit procedural decisions. Size relates to the overall quantity of information in the audit trail, measured either as the number of interviews, amount of filed information, or number of pages. A study with 100 pages of interview notes has different implications for the audit than does a study with 500 pages of interview notes, 200 pages of observational records, and 100 documents. Size affects the time required to conduct the audit as well as the auditor's sampling decisions.

The methodology of the study will also affect audit decisions. When evaluation design decisions continue to evolve, and when many different data sources and analytic strategies are used, the audit tasks may be very complex. A more dynamic, interactive, and emergent evaluation design will be more difficult to audit than will a preordinate design because the evaluator is required to make (and, therefore, document) many more decisions during the inquiry. Thus, there are more records for an auditor to scrutinize and more possibilities for otherwise unnoticed errors and biases to occur.

Determine How the
Available Time Will
Affect the Audit

The amount of time available to spend on the audit may of necessity be predetermined. This amount may be confined by a budget or by a fixed deadline. If so, both the scope and procedures will be affected. Audit objectives will have to be defined within the constraints of the time available, and, at least potentially, shortcuts may have to be made in the procedures. The auditor must balance the need for a timely audit report against the need to conduct a thorough examination. He or she may decide that it is impossible to perform an adequate audit in the time available.

Determine Whether the Early
Involvement of the Auditor
Will Affect the Audit

Our primary interest is in the auditor as a summative metaevaluator who attests to evaluation quality once an evaluation has been completed.

When it is known that an audit will be desirable or necessary, an auditee may contact an auditor prior to the start of the study to provide assistance in setting up the audit trail. The auditee may then call another auditor when the evaluation is complete, or retain the services of the first auditor. If the auditor who contributes to the design of the audit trail is the same auditor who is later called upon to render an attestation, it may be argued that there is a potential conflict of interest. It may be that this auditor has been coopted or has become an interested party, thereby sacrificing independence and objectivity. We think that this is unlikely, provided that once the auditor helps establish the audit trail, he or she ceases involvement with the study until it is completed.

If the auditor continues to be involved in providing advice during the study, he or she begins functioning as an internal auditor or formative metaevaluator. This role is really more closely aligned with that of a peer debriefer or consultant than that of an independent, third-party examiner. Involvement of the auditor after the inquiry is completed is the major role we see for the auditor, and the only one that really provides an outside readership with the ever important attest function.

Determine How the Auditor's
Background Characteristics
Will Affect the Audit

The auditor's background will play a major role in the quality of the audit, in particular his or her familiarity with the substantive issues involved in the evaluation, experience as an auditor, and overall methodological expertise. The substantive area under investigation is relevant because an unfamiliar evaluand or setting may mean that more time is required for the auditor to become oriented. On the other hand, a lack of familiarity may create the necessary distance for the auditor to remain objective and less likely to judge the outcomes in accord with his or her own prior knowledge. In general, some familiarity with the evaluand and setting is preferred because it informs the auditor's judgment, particularly with regard to the subtle tacit analytic techniques, potentially unrecognized by one unfamiliar with the substantive issues.

Prior experience in naturalistic evaluation and in auditing will affect the amount of time required to audit and the depth of the examination. Perhaps more importantly, experience in methodology and in auditing will enhance the auditor's ability to audit the data analytic processes efficiently. Experience will also make the auditor more attuned to common biases, as well as to judging what is an "acceptable" amount of bias.

The role relationship between the auditee and auditor is also important. They must form a working relationship based upon collaboration and trust, lest the audit be perceived as a threat, rather than a contribution. We suggest that auditee and auditor have a similar professional status to prevent possible power conflicts, and to prevent conflicts arising from differences in experiences. Finally, as noted in Chapter 2, the auditor should have no stake in the outcomes of the evaluation.

Discuss Audit Scope,
Objectives, and Standards

Once the auditor has become acquainted with the nature of the evaluation in question and is familiar with the strengths and shortcomings of the audit trail, he or she should review with the auditee the proposed scope of the audit examination, its objectives, and the criteria or standards to be applied in rendering an attestation. In the illustration provided in this chapter, we assume the following: (1) The auditor and auditee have agreed that the audit will require examining evaluation procedures and findings, (2) to determine whether the evaluation met the criteria of confirmability, dependability, and credibility, (3) as defined by Lincoln and Guba (Guba, 1981; Lincoln & Guba, 1985) for naturalistic inquiries. (Different audit objectives and standards are discussed in Chapter 6.)

The auditor may feel that certain adjustments are required in the audit trail in order to proceed with the proposed audit objectives. For example, the auditor may ask the evaluator to decipher shorthand codes used in field notes. An evaluator may have tape recorded all interviews and then prepared notes directly from the tapes. If there is not sufficient time for the auditor to listen to all the tapes, he or she may ask the evaluator to transcribe several tapes so that the condensed notes can be more easily checked against the raw data. The auditee must decide whether these adjustments can be made.

Both auditor and auditee should have a clear understanding of the standards to be used by the auditor in rendering an attestation. By stating explicitly what can and cannot be done, there will be little room for disagreement or disappointment when the auditor's examination is completed.

Before entering into a formal agreement, the auditor and auditee should discuss the logistical arrangements required for access to the audit trail files. This is particularly important when geographical distance separates the auditor from auditee. The auditee may not want to release the irreplaceable materials for fear of losing them, losing immediate access to them, or violating confidentiality through the loan of interview transcripts. Although this may be resolved by making multiple copies, it is preferable for the auditor to make an on-site visit. The auditor is in a potentially threatening position, and must act in a sensitive manner when making logistical arrangements. The auditee may want some reassurances as to what the auditor plans to do and may not want to let the data and audit trail get too far away. Whatever arrangements are made, it is best for the alternatives to be discussed during the negotiations.

FORMALIZING THE CONTRACT

A contract or letter of agreement between the auditee and auditor will help to manage expectations and role relationships during the audit. A contract established at the beginning of the audit is highly recommended. The interdependence of the auditee, the audit trail, and the auditor will require the cooperation and collaboration of both parties throughout the audit. Although the contract may be written or oral, we recommend a written contract to ensure that the parties are in agreement from the beginning through the duration. A written contract need not suggest an inflexible audit examination. The issue of flexibility can be addressed by integrating renegotiation criteria into the contract. A mechanism for feedback and ongoing communications and for facilitating possible renegotiation is important in a contract because as the auditor becomes more familiar with the evaluation, the assumptions brought to the task may change (Leitzman et al., 1980; Walter & Earle, 1981-1982).

The written contract or verbal project agreement should include a number of areas: (1) audit objectives, (2) the form of the final report, (3) method of payment, (4) time line, (5) roles and expectations, (6) logistics, (7) assurance of the auditor's credentials, (8) audit criteria/ standards, and (9) renegotiation criteria.

Specify Audit Objectives

As noted in Chapter 2, an evaluation can be audited along several dimensions. Specification of objectives is critical because the objectives shape the scope of the audit examination. In the present example, the audit objectives are to attest to the trustworthiness or rigor of the evaluation process and product. The work program described in Event D on Table 5.1 has been designed to achieve these audit objectives.

Identify Form of the
Final Audit Report

The final audit report must serve the needs of the auditee. The contractual agreement should spell out what the deliverable product(s) will be. Possibilities include a two paragraph, short-form statement of attestation, a several-page statement of auditor findings, or a long-form (10 pages or more) statement that includes findings, audit methods used, and examples that shaped the conclusions. (See Chapter 3 for a more complete description of these options.)

Determine Method of Payment

The agreement should include some statement about payment for the audit. It may be made as a professional fee, or through a quid pro quo arrangement. If the payment is offered as a fixed-fee for the audit (as opposed to hourly), the auditor should ascertain as closely as possible how long the audit will take. This estimate can be based largely upon the auditability assessment and the expectations for the final report.

Establish Time Line

If the evaluator needs the final audit report by a certain date, the auditor will have to estimate how long the audit will take, and arrange, as part of the agreement, to set a fixed date when the audit must begin. The formality of this is important to ensure the auditor does not find him- or herself in a position of having to deliver an audit report with less time than he or she feels is appropriate. It also protects the interests of the auditee who needs a timely audit report. The auditee may be in a contract situation in which a deliverable is required on a fixed date. The auditor will want to be in a position to schedule the necessary amount of time to complete the audit process.

Specify Roles and Expectations

Specifying roles and explaining what the audit can and cannot do will help set the ground rules and establish clarity of the commitments to the audit by both the auditor and auditee. Role specification will also help to clarify the way in which the auditor and auditee will interact. It may be important for the auditor to have access to the auditee to answer questions. It will be important for the auditor to have assurance that the auditee will not interfere with access to the audit trail. Finally, it may be important for the auditee to provide verbal feedback prior to a written report, or to negotiate issues of missing data or other problems in the audit trail.

Arrange Logistics

This simply refers to specifying how, when, and where the auditor will be given access to the audit trail materials.

Assure Auditor's Credentials

The auditee and users of the audit report may want or need some assurance of the auditor's credentials. Although this may not be necessary to include in a written contract, auditor qualifications will have to be established before either the auditee or prospective information users will value the audit. As noted earlier, the auditor should be a competent methodologist and have prior knowledge of the type of evaluation and substantive issues under consideration. An evaluator may choose to seek sponsors' or information users' approval of the auditor by sharing the auditor's credentials with them. If these individuals are not assured of the auditor's competence, the quality of the audit may be irrelevant.

Specify Audit Standards/Criteria

Both auditor and auditee must clearly understand the standards or criteria to be used by the auditor in rendering an attestation. In the present example, both parties must subscribe to the view that attesting to the fairness or trustworthiness of the evaluation involves an examination of whether procedures and findings were confirmable, dependable, and credible (as defined by Guba, 1981; Lincoln & Guba,

1985). Other criteria could also be used as standards for qualitative, interpretive studies. These include the criteria and strategies described by LeCompte and Goetz (1982) and Goetz and LeCompte (1984) for establishing reliability and validity of ethnographic studies and Dawson's (1980) or Kennedy's (1984) approach to demonstrating the validity of qualitative data. What is important is that the evaluator subscribes to a particular point of view, that the auditor is thoroughly familiar with that point of view, and that the audit work program be designed to examine or attest to the use of the standards or criteria in question.

Identify Renegotiation Criteria

It is always useful to have the opportunity to renegotiate if and when unforeseen events occur. The fact that both parties agree to this philosophy and to the types of things that may be renegotiated should be included in the formal agreement.

PREPARING AND IMPLEMENTING A WORK PROGRAM TO DETERMINE TRUSTWORTHINESS

As discussed in Chapter 2, the auditor's work program should specify what procedures he or she will follow to achieve the audit objectives. The auditor then implements the work program by actually gathering and evaluating evidence to test the auditee's claims. We have combined these steps and prepared a work program for determining the trustworthiness of a naturalistic evaluation.

The work program is constructed in such a way that it facilitates the auditor's evaluation of the claims made by the auditee. In the context of auditing a naturalistic evaluation for trustworthiness, an auditor is attesting to three claims about the evaluation procedures and products:

(1) The findings are dependable. That is, the procedures used to gather, analyze, and interpret the data adhere to generally accepted practices for naturalistic evaluation.
(2) The findings are confirmable. That is, findings are supported in the data and inferences made in reaching conclusions were not illogical or unreasonable.
(3) Appropriate action was taken to ensure credible findings. That is, the findings were perceived as credible by those who participated in the study.

The work program is used to gather evidence to form a professional opinion on whether these claims are reasonable; in other words the auditor attests to the reasonableness and dependability of the auditee's assertions about the evaluation. At the conclusion of the audit examination, the auditor prepares a report, which contains his or her opinion.

In planning a work program, the auditor identifies the major audit objectives to be addressed (i.e., the auditee's claims), reviews the literature in accepted practices, develops focusing questions for guiding the audit examination, and specifies accepted principles to be used as standards or criteria for the attestation. In our example, Sections D-7, D-8, and D-9 in Table 5.1 address audit objectives and list focusing questions that map back to evidence in the audit trail. The "Events" in column 1 specify the accepted criteria for determining trustworthiness. The following discussion summarizes information presented in the table under Events, Auditor Tasks, and Focusing Questions. Selected focusing questions are elaborated on as an aid to the auditor.

Assess Confirmability

In making an examination of confirmability, the auditor attempts to judge the inquirer's neutrality in interpreting events and descriptions (Guba, 1981). To make this judgment the auditor assesses whether: (1) the findings are grounded in the data, (2) the inferences are logical, (3) the category structure is useful, and (4) the inquirer acknowledged, accounted for, and accommodated divergencies and discrepancies in the data.

Assess Whether the Findings Are Grounded in the Data

The auditor must determine whether the evaluation findings and conclusions are supported by the data. The objective here is to verify that each finding shows evidence of having originated in the evaluation in question, and that it has evolved throughout the data analytic process. At this stage, the auditor is not judging the importance of any single datum or related finding, but simply verifying its existence and history within the context of the study.

The assessment of whether findings are grounded in the data involves the auditor in four tasks: (1) sampling findings, (2) identifying audit trail files linked to each finding, (3) verifying the linkage between audit trail files and findings, and (4) assessing the incidence of undisciplined subjectivity. Critical considerations involved in all of these tasks are discussed below.

Sampling. Depending upon the size and complexity of the evaluation and the time available to complete the audit, the auditor may choose to track every finding or to select and track only a subset of findings. Factors that will affect sampling decisions include: (a) number of pages of raw notes, (b) number of transcribed interviews, (c) number of pages of audit trail, (d) time span of the study, (e) number of days (weeks) between initial contact and final report, (f) number of methodological techniques, and (g) frequency of shifting methods.

There is no optimal audit sampling strategy; both purposive and random sampling may be appropriate. Purposive or judgmental sampling may be preferred when there are potentially controversial findings in the evaluation report; when findings contradict what is known from evaluations of similar evaluands in similar contexts, or when the auditor has reason to believe that findings may be influenced by political pressures. In these cases, an auditor might select only those findings that will matter most to information users; that is, those most likely to be debated, considered to be controversial, and so forth. When an auditor chooses to sample purposively by selecting only those findings regarded as most important or critical and is unable to track an important finding to the raw data, the assessment of confirmability may emerge as a top priority for the audit examination. In this case, the auditor would likely want to check each and every finding for confirmability. If findings are not confirmable, it makes little sense to proceed with an examination of dependability.

Random sampling may be appropriate when none of the conditions listed above obtain and when there is a very large number of findings to be checked. A random sample of findings could be drawn and checked under the assumption that if this sample of findings is supported in the data, then all other findings will be supported as well. A random sampling strategy may also be used in the following situation: An evaluator has collected all data on audiotape and then prepared summary sheets of key points from the tapes, skipping the step of transcribing the tapes. From an auditor's point of view, the audit will be expedited if he or she can rely on the summary sheets as a source of raw data rather than having to listen to all of the audiotapes. The auditor may want to listen to a random sample of tapes to determine whether the summary sheets accurately reflect the raw data on the tape. If, on the basis of this test, the auditor is satisfied as to the accuracy and completeness of the summary sheets, he or she may conclude that it will suffice to use the summary sheets as a source of raw data for the audit.

Mapping findings to data. As part of the effort to determine whether the findings are grounded in the data, the auditor should track the transformation of raw data into analyzed, then synthesized, data. The auditor should also determine whether each datum is given the proper weight or emphasis. Through the cross-references, the auditor should follow each finding back to its evolving states until he or she reaches the raw data from which it was initially generated. This task is relatively straightforward when there are cross-reference codes on the statements of findings and analyzed data that map back to the raw data.

Relative weighting of the data. When tracking the data transformation, the auditor should look at the terminology used by the auditee in the statements of findings. Words such as *many,* or *most,* versus *several, few,* or *none* suggest more than just a tracking task from an idea to a data point. In an interview study for example, these words suggest that a quantity of respondents hold to a particular belief or have a particular concern. The auditor should verify the prevalence of the concern.

Imposition of the evaluator's own terminology in the data. One expects that the naturalistic evaluator will represent the inquiry situation from the perspective of respondents or stakeholders. In cases in which the evaluator does not describe phenomena in the terminology of the respondents, the auditor might be concerned that the evaluator imposed his or her own preconceived notions on the interpretation of the evaluand, thereby not being true to the respondents or the data.

The auditor addresses this by reading through the evaluation proposal, examining entries in the evaluator's personal log, recalling earlier conversations with the auditee about the study, and looking for terminology or jargon used. Next, the auditor examines the raw data to see if that jargon appears there. If it does, it may suggest that the evaluator may have prematurely translated respondent perceptions into an interpretation or framework that reflects what the evaluator brought to the study, not what the evaluator learned from the respondents. In short, this examination is an attempt to determine whether the framework or perspective brought to the study by the evaluator has played too strong a role in shaping the outcomes. The auditor may also judge whether the perspective or inquiry framework displayed in the evaluation proposal seemed to set boundaries for the findings prematurely.

Assess Whether Inferences Are Logical

Assessing the logic of inferences is an intuitive, subjective process. Naturalistic evaluators will not reduce their data into a series of logic statements or propositions. So how can the auditor really judge the logic employed by the auditee? If the auditor is sufficiently familiar with the substantive issues under consideration in the evaluation, it may be easier to grasp the elegance or flaws in inference. In cases in which the auditor is not familiar with these issues, he or she may have to scrutinize more carefully the processes used by the evaluator to transform raw data into categories, themes and interpretations.

The challenge is to understand the mental leaps made by the evaluator when making inferences. It is not an easy task for the auditor to unravel the evaluator's complex cognitive process. One way the auditor may proceed is to approximate the inferential processes by studying the evaluator's data reduction rules and how precisely the rules were followed. Auditors are concerned about whether efforts to make sense of raw data and to impose some structure on it are fair or reasonable. Although the auditor is obligated to make a judgment, we must recall that the auditor provides only a professional opinion on this matter, not a guarantee.

In assessing whether the auditee's inferences are logical, the auditor (1) identifies the analytic strategies used by the auditee, (2) assesses the applications of those strategies, (3) assesses the accuracy of the descriptions of the phenomena, concepts, and issues under investigation, and (4) determines whether inferences are unsubstantiated or illogical. Major considerations in accomplishing these tasks are discussed below.

Use of analytic technique and selection of unit of analysis. If we agree that assessing the logic of an inference is difficult, it may help to look at the evaluator's strategies when analyzing data and drawing inferences and then determine their appropriateness.

As Goetz and LeCompte (1981) point out, analytic techniques vary widely and inquirers generally use a number of procedures in an overlapping fashion in any given study. They identify five generally accepted strategies including: (1) analytic induction (cf. Lindesmith, 1947), (2) the constant comparative method (cf. Glaser & Strauss, 1967), (3) typological analysis (cf. Lofland, 1971), (4) enumerative systems (cf. Denzin, 1978), and (5) standardized observational protocols (cf. Dunkin & Biddle, 1974). Furthermore, the ways in which data are subjected to analysis vary widely (Miles & Huberman, 1984). In some cases, data are reduced after they are all collected. In most naturalistic evaluations, data analysis will occur throughout the evaluation. An auditor should investigate the various strategies employed by the auditee and learn how and when they were used during the evaluation.

For the purpose of simplifying the discussion of the auditor's role here, we have organized the data analysis and synthesis processes into five general stages: (1) identifying categories, (2) developing categories, (3) establishing relationships between categories, (4) establishing relationships to existing research, and (5) presenting the outcomes. The auditor will examine the development of categories, the precision of the terminology used to describe categories, and the consistency of the selected units of analysis across the raw data, the findings, and the final report. Categories may be descriptive or conceptual. For example, in an organizational study, descriptive categories may be groups, departments, centers, divisions, and so forth; conceptual categories may include centralization, formalization, reward structure, span of control, authority, power, and so forth. In this type of study, relationships between categories may show, for example, that the reward structure changes as one moves up the organizational hierarchy, or that individual power is related to budget control. As the evaluator works with the data, he or she will be trying to identify an optimal set of categories to describe the evaluand. As behaviors, events, concerns, and issues are observed, the evaluator will try to classify them in accordance with the category structure being developed. The auditor should be alert to the fact that categories are likely to evolve and change to accommodate new information. Categories will likely be labeled with a code. Auditors must understand the coding scheme in order to track the data analysis process.

The determination of inferential logic requires an examination of whether categories reflect the working hypotheses, and must take into account whether there are unused data. The auditor should expect to see working hypotheses followed up and reflected in the findings, and should expect to find a statement of a rationale for excluding any working hypotheses and data.

Categories and emerging working hypotheses. The auditor will verify that the audit trail shows the relationship between the derived categories comprising the findings and the emerging working hypotheses found in the theoretical notes. The category scheme displayed in the findings presumably represents the final version of the data in its clearest, most elegant form. The auditor should expect to see how the categorical structure evolved during the study. For example, working hypotheses would be identified and described in the audit trail. The audit trail should show how the evaluator explored these working hypotheses and how new data either confirmed, disconfirmed, or modified the emerging categories of findings.

Alternative explanations. The assumption of multiple realities (Lincoln & Guba, 1985) allows for multiple plausible interpretations of the data. Thus it makes little sense for the auditor to reanalyze the data. However, the auditor can attest to whether the interpretive framework developed by the evaluator is supported by the data. If findings are not substantiated in the data or if conclusions seem illogical, the audit report should reflect that fact.

In cases in which the auditor assesses all conclusions for logical relations to the data, a conclusion that is illogically derived may prompt an interaction between the auditor and evaluator. The auditor may suggest that a modification of the conclusion would be more accurate in view of the data. Or, the auditor may report that, in his or her professional judgment, the conclusion overstates what the data support. If the conclusion is changed as the result of conversations with the auditor, it is appropriate for that to be documented either in the body of the evaluation report or in the auditor's report.

In cases in which the conclusions were sampled, and one or more is speculative, the unsampled conclusions will likely be held suspect as well. The auditor may then have to expand the scope of the examination to include a review of all conclusions.

Assess the Utility
of the Category Structure

The category structure is the scheme developed by the evaluator to tie the major concepts and findings together. One may argue that this scheme is better evaluated by the user of the evaluation report than by the auditor. However, the auditor may evaluate the clarity, fair representation, and explanatory power of the category structure.

The auditor may decide whether an optimal set of categories has been selected from the data by ascertaining whether they are useful in helping to describe the evaluand and context. Explanatory power is evident when a concise framework and category structure ties together and explains a large number of events, issues, concerns, and so forth. (This is analogous to a statistical study when a few variables explain most of the variance.) The category structure is useful when the reader perceives it as elegant and when it helps the reader understand the outcomes. When there are many overlapping categories without a clear explanation, the findings may seem fuzzy or confusing to the reader. (A clear presentation of the findings is a major responsibility of the evaluator.) In cases in which the categories are unclear, the data may support the findings, but the findings may not help explain the evaluand. In assessing utility, the auditor (1) examines the clarity of the category structure, (2) assesses its explanatory power, and (3) assesses the fit between categories, definitions, and examples. Obtaining answers to several guiding questions (see Table 5.1, D-7.c) should help the auditor make this assessment.

Descriptive power of category labels. Because the basic interpretive framework derived during the evaluation will eventually drive the reader's understanding of the evaluand under investigation, it is important that category labels used be accurate descriptors of the items comprising that particular category.

Explanatory power of categories. Normally, in a final evaluation report, an evaluator will portray categories of relevant findings, explain the significance of the category, and illustrate the finding with one or more examples. These examples may be anecdotes, excerpts from interviews, and other portrayals of qualitative data. The auditor may choose to focus on verifying the examples that are used to illustrate the categories.

Assess Whether the Evaluator
Accounted for Discrepant Data

Discrepant data refer to those data that do not quite fit the fabric of the evolving interpretation. They may not be as pronounced as some of the other data; they may argue against the evaluator's lines of thinking.

The auditor's task here is to learn how the auditee dealt with contradictory data. Through triangulation, the auditee collects data from multiple sources to see whether data converge, thereby raising his or her confidence level about the accuracy of the data. But what if the data do not converge? The auditor must look through the theoretical notes, data reconstruction notes, and process notes to determine (1) what rules of analysis were used, and (2) how data that did not quite fit the emerging framework were treated. The quality of the auditor's assessment of this aspect of confirmability will largely depend on the clarity of the descriptions in the audit trail. The files should show, for example, that in attempting to reach closure and saturation, the evaluator modified emerging findings as new data were uncovered. Table 5.1 (Event D-7.d) lists two focusing questions to help the auditor make this assessment.

Assess Dependability

The dependability assessment is more directly observable through the audit trail than is a confirmability assessment because the processes an auditee follows are easier to document than are the inferences the auditee makes. Using the appropriate audit trail files, it is a relatively straightforward task for the auditor to examine the auditee's decisions about who to interview, how a key informant was chosen, how long to stay on site, the criteria used to bound the inquiry, how to analyze the data, and so forth.

In making an examination of dependability, the auditor attempts to assess acceptable and consistent methodological practice (Guba, 1981; Lincoln & Guba, 1985). To gauge consistency, the auditor should judge the overall quality of the evaluation design and the ongoing methodological decisions to ascertain how the design and implementation promoted consistency. To make this judgment, the auditor assesses whether (1) the inquiry decisions and methodological shifts were appropriate, and (2) the evaluator was biased and made obvious errors in judgment.

Assess the Appropriateness
of the Inquiry Decisions and
Methodological Shifts

The need for a dependability audit of the evaluation process arises because of the emergent design employed in a naturalistic evaluation. In this type of design, "succeeding methodological steps are based upon the results of steps already taken. . . . At times only simple refinements in procedure or a simple adjustment in questions may be called for, but at other times an investigator may strike out on a wholly new tack as a result of a single insight" (Lincoln & Guba, 1985, pp. 102-103). To demonstrate the dependability of this evaluation design and the process by which it was implemented, the evaluator (auditee) maintains a record of his or her evolving methodological decisions. The auditor examines this record to attest to dependability.

Relationship between sampling decisions and working hypotheses. An auditor will be interested in inquiry decisions that involve the use of purposive (Lincoln & Guba, 1985) or theoretical sampling (Glaser & Strauss, 1967). This type of sampling is emergent, involves serial selection of sampling units, and is continually adjusted to accommodate the evaluator's developing insights and working hypotheses. It is probable that sampling will stop when no new data are discovered that alter the categories used to explain the evaluand. Glaser and Strauss (1967) refer to this as reaching "theoretical saturation":

> Saturation means that no additional data are being found whereby the [investigator] can develop properties of the category. As he sees similar instances over and over again, the researcher becomes empirically confident that a category is saturated. (p. 61)

An auditor will be concerned with the degree to which this decision is logical, reasonable, and appropriate for the evaluation.

Decisions about whom to sample should be observable in the audit trail. The auditor should find in the audit trail evidence of the relationship between the working hypotheses and purposive sampling decisions. It should be clear how each decision relates to the need to collect more data relative to the evolving interpretation. For example, the evidence may show that a respondent introduced a new idea that steered the evaluator to a particular individual or document to support or refute some claim. The auditor would expect to see evidence that the evaluator responded to a particular information need when the situation called for it. Without this evidence of the auditee's ongoing working hypotheses and methodological choices, an auditor would be concerned about the dependability of the inquiry.

Assess the Degree and
Incidence of Evaluator Bias

Evaluator bias is very difficult to guard against, and attesting to a successful effort is one of the most crucial functions of the audit. The auditor may evaluate the strategies used to control bias by (1) identifying decisions for bounding the inquiry, (2) looking for instances that may suggest cooptation, (3) identifying whether ungrounded judgments were made, (4) assessing the possibility of a Pygmalion effect, (5) looking for evidence of a Hawthorne effect, and (6) examining methods for triangulation. The auditor will need to make determinations about each of these potential biases by carefully studying the audit trail documentation. Several symptoms of bias are discussed below.

Evidence of early closure. The auditor should review the theoretical notes, methodological notes, and notes about intentions to understand the forces influencing the evaluator's perceptions and actions during the evaluation. For example, the auditor should look for evidence showing that the evaluation may have been prematurely completed to meet a deadline. The auditor should look for evidence to decide whether the evaluator lacked flexibility as a result of political pressures on site.

Unexplored areas in the field notes. Evidence of decisions to set boundaries to the evaluation will be evident in the evaluator's decisions of what not to include in the findings. Although the auditor's primary goal is not to reanalyze the field notes for themes, he or she may incidentally find evidence of issues that are identified but not explored further, yet seem relevant. These may be issues that alter the direction of the study or clearly contradict the reported findings. Although the evaluator may bound the inquiry such that said area(s) are excluded, the auditor should be able to find some rationale for their exclusion.

Adherence to an interview schedule. Strict adherence to an interview schedule is not a problem per se. However, the auditor should look for evidence that interview schedules did not foreclose on finding new information, and that the evaluator was willing to modify interview schedules to follow new leads. In a naturalistic evaluation, the evaluator learns, follows leads, and probes into new areas as dictated by earlier findings. Thus the auditor would expect to find evidence that as the state of knowledge changed over time, new questions were introduced to reflect that fact. If no changes are found, it suggests that perhaps the evaluator never strayed from the ideas held at the beginning of the study. The auditor might in turn conclude that the boundaries for the inquiry were prematurely set at the beginning of the study.

Search for negative cases. An auditor may become suspicious if all of the data collected during the inquiry seem to fall neatly and predictably into an interpretation. The evaluator is responsible for attempts to disprove his or her interpretations of the evaluand and to explore alternative hypotheses and interpretations. Negative examples should be used to redefine evolving interpretations (Goetz & LeCompte, 1981; Lincoln & Guba, 1985). Thus, an auditor would normally expect to find evidence of both methodological shifts and evolving interpretations. As a way to verify that closure was not premature, the auditor should also expect to find evidence that the evaluator consciously attempted to disprove his or her evolving perspective.

Identification with figure(s) of authority. In assessing the possibility of evaluator cooptation, the auditor should look for evidence that findings and interpretations reflect all stakeholders' concerns. If the evaluator seems to have spent a disproportionate amount of time with one or a few key individuals, it is important to determine to what degree the data and findings may reflect too small a subset of stakeholders. Perhaps the pattern of associations shows that one or more key people in positions of authority or power had frequent interactions with others. If so, it may suggest that the key figures are trying to obtain information about the investigation, or to influence information discussed by other respondents.

Shifts in feelings of empathy. Another area for examination is reference in the audit trail files to the evaluator's values and feelings and awareness of these feelings. The auditor should attempt to learn how the feelings and values described in the audit trail (personal notes) influence the evaluation and how they change during the course of the inquiry. It is important to determine whether values or feelings of empathy have made the evaluator more attentive to some groups than to others.

Support for methodological choices. An auditor is interested in whether the evaluator made sound, defensible methodological choices. One way to track this is by looking through the personal notes to see whether they play too large a role in the analysis or in the methodological shifts. Ungrounded judgments may be indicated by the fact that feelings more than facts dictate the direction of the evaluation.

Use of preliminary evaluation questions. As part of the auditor's assessment of whether the evaluator has fallen prey to a Pygmalion effect, the auditor must decide whether the evaluator has projected himself or herself too much into what is being observed. This bias may influence the evaluation during data collection or during data analysis. If, during data collection, field notes (i.e., interview notes) are prepared only after filtering or interpretation has taken place, this may reflect evaluator predispositions rather than respondent perceptions. In data analysis, the auditor must examine whether the evaluator was particularly sensitive to data supporting his or her predispositions. One way for the auditor to assess this incidence of bias is to look at the data and findings to see if they map back to the preliminary questions of the study. This examination, in combination with a review of the personal notes, may make it possible to detect whether ideas in the mind of the evaluator at the onset of the evaluation may have been sustained throughout the study despite the fact that data may have been collected that contradicts these ideas.

Similarity in language. It is also within the purview of the auditor to determine whether the evaluator has created a Hawthorne effect. This bias may be evident in the wording of interview questions or in the actual field notes. If notes from interviews display the same language as appears in the proposal for the study, this may indicate that respondents were providing answers that they expected the evaluator wanted to hear. The auditor may also look for evidence of a Hawthorne effect by listening to audiotapes or viewing videotapes of observations. It may be possible to detect nonverbal cues or subtle intonations in evaluator questions that prompted the respondent to answer in a manner desired by the evaluator (Sebeok & Rosenthal, 1981).

Appearance of naiveté. Through the auditee's reflexive notes and other personal notes, it may be possible to recognize the effects of a naive evaluator. Understandably, the personal note reflections of a novice and expert will vary (see, e.g., Reinharz, 1979). The novice is likely to record more about his or her emotional state than will an experienced evaluator. A more experienced evaluator will likely have been through many of these same introspections, thus find them less striking, and possibly not significant enough to record.

Evidence of triangulation. Sound practice for naturalistic evaluation involves the use of triangulation (of investigators, methods, perspectives, etc., Denzin, 1978). Therefore, the auditor should expect to find evidence of triangulation strategies in the auditee's process notes. The auditor should also expect to see confirmation of working hypotheses only after the auditee has engaged in triangulation. When working hypotheses are confirmed in the absence of such efforts, it suggests the evaluator did not systematically set out to either confirm or disprove them.

Review Credibility

As noted in Chapter 4, credibility refers to the truth value of the evaluation findings (Guba, 1981; Lincoln & Guba, 1985). Unlike either dependability or confirmability for which auditing is the primary quality assurance strategy, credibility may be assured through a variety of other techniques. Lincoln and Guba (1985) describe several procedures to enhance credibility including triangulation, prolonged engagement, peer debriefing, negative case analysis, referential adequacy, and member checking. Since these techniques are among the generally accepted practices for naturalistic evaluators, a credibility audit is not really necessary to demonstrate or attest to this aspect of an evaluation. However, it does seem reasonable for the auditor, who is already intimately familiar with the audit trail, to verify that efforts to ensure credibility were undertaken. Reviewing credibility involves (1) examining the design and implementation of credibility strategies, and (2) reviewing the impact of credibility strategies on methodological choices, data sources, and findings.

Review the Design and Implementation
of Credibility Strategies

Efforts to ensure credibility will normally be described in the final report. If so, the auditor's role may be one of verifying that the explanation about credibility is accurate, given the evidence in the audit trail. For example, the final report may describe how the evaluator triangulated data sources and methods, conducted member checks, debriefed with peers, engaged in negative case analysis, and was engaged on site for an appropriate length of time. Having access to the audit trail, the auditor is clearly in a position to read about these techniques and to evaluate whether they were implemented in an appropriate manner.

Review the Impact of
Credibility Strategies

Naturalistic inquirers rely on the strategy of using multiple data sources and methods and attempt to verify findings by presenting them to peers and to respondents. The hope is that findings converge, thereby raising the evaluator's confidence that the findings are credible. But, what if the information and feedback from various sources do not converge? What strategies are followed to explain the lack of convergence?

Typically, when describing triangulation, the final report will present the outcomes of that process. However, the auditor will have access to the audit trail to review the degree to which there was corroboration across sources and convergence of findings across methods, and he or she should be prepared to attest to how thorough the evaluator was in applying the credibility strategies.

PREPARING THE AUDIT REPORT

In the last stage of the audit, the auditor prepares a report including an opinion about the trustworthiness of the evaluation. The nature and forms of the reporting should be in accord with the negotiated agreement. Chapter 3 provides additional detail on preparing an audit report. In the present example, the body of the report would include:

- Statement of purpose: description of the general purpose of the audit in the context of the naturalistic evaluation in question; identification of auditee, evaluand, context and setting.
- Statement of scope: explanation of what the auditor examined (e.g., findings, types of files, records of procedures) including any restrictions, constraints, or limitations on the examination; an explanation of confirmability, dependability, and credibility used as standards for the attestation.

- Statement of findings: the auditor's opinion on the auditee's performance in view of each of the three standards described above.

Feedback and Renegotiation

The major outcome of the auditor's examination is a statement of findings about the evaluation process and products. Although the audit may have been commissioned by the evaluator solely for his or her own benefit, we are primarily concerned with situations in which the auditor's opinion is rendered for the benefit of information users. In either situation, it is important for the auditor to discuss audit findings prior to issuing a final report. This discussion is equivalent to a member check used by the evaluator to enhance the likelihood of reporting valid findings. It will provide an opportunity for the auditee to dispute the audit outcomes if necessary and to evaluate the integrity of the audit methods used.

If the auditee points out a flaw in the auditor's judgment, for example that crucial evidence was overlooked, the auditor should weigh the new evidence in light of his or her initial finding. However, if the evaluator disagrees with the auditor's finding, he or she may choose to rebut the finding by marshaling supporting evidence.

Complete Agreement

Typically, an auditor's report will appear as an addendum to the final evaluation report. Minimally, the audit report should conform to the standards agreed upon in the negotiation of the contract discussed earlier. The evaluator (auditee) must decide whether the report satisfies his or her objectives in having the study audited.

SUMMARY

This chapter has presented a procedure for conducting an audit and has explained one specific application—that of attesting to the trustworthiness of naturalistic evaluations. It expanded upon the general auditing procedure introduced in Chapter 2 by describing the tasks necessary to complete this type of audit including, preparing for an audit, assessing auditability, negotiating and formalizing the contract, preparing and implementing a work program, and preparing an audit report. As an aid in developing an audit work program, the chapter also discussed a number of focusing questions that guide the auditor's procedures and direct him or her to relevant records in the audit trail. Although we acknowledge that the procedure has some practical limitations, we argue that adhering to the procedures will ultimately help the auditor provide a more informed and justifiable opinion about the trustworthiness of the evaluation processes and outcomes.

EXERCISES

1. Imagine you received a call from a professional acquaintance to conduct an audit of an evaluation for a price of $200 per day, and for a maximum of $1,200. What questions would you ask? What would you do first? How would you decide whether or not to take the job?

2. Describe how you would proceed if someone commissioned you to conduct an audit. Describe how you would proceed when determining auditability. What auditability criteria would you use? How would you decide whether the criteria were met? How would you determine whether you selected the right ones? What would make you relatively certain that you could complete the audit in the time allowed?

3. In what ways do you think that auditing a study could contribute to your own professional growth as an evaluator?

4. You are conducting an audit. After reading the final evaluation report, you begin to track the findings for support in the raw data. The audit trail is fairly well cross-referenced, yet you cannot find very much data to support some of the findings. What will you do next?

5. After talking to the auditee whose study you are auditing, you suspect that he or she has been heavily influenced by a particular stakeholder. How would you go about trying to find out whether this may have biased the study? What records will you review? How will you decide whether the evaluator was biased?

6. You are a graduate student who has agreed to audit a fellow graduate student's doctoral dissertation for aspects of trustworthiness. You know the auditee is anxious to finish his study and to complete his Ph.D. requirements. In fact, he has scheduled his defense, and you have not yet begun the audit. The dissertation is to be submitted 10 days from today, and you are told that you can begin your audit in six days. How will you design your work program? What special considerations (if any) will you make because this is an audit of a dissertation study? What special considerations (if any) will you make because of the four-day limitation? What are your alternatives?

6

Developing Other Applications

Previous chapters have illustrated the use of auditing as a model for metaevaluation—the evaluation of evaluation. Chapters 1, 2, and 3 provided a general framework for understanding the links between auditing and metaevaluation. Chapters 4 and 5 discussed the development of both an audit trail and an audit work program from the perspective of auditing a naturalistic evaluation for trustworthiness. We do not wish to leave readers with the impression that auditing, as a tool for metaevaluation, can be used only in naturalistic evaluation. This chapter offers some suggestions for developing an audit trail and audit work program, given: (1) a focus for naturalistic inquiry other than evaluation, (2) an inquiry paradigm other than naturalistic inquiry, and (3) a set of evaluation audit objectives other than determining trustworthiness. This chapter offers only suggestions and guidance for these situations; no attempt is made to develop an audit approach on the scale of the previous two chapters.

AUDITING OTHER NATURALISTIC INQUIRIES

In Chapter 4 we noted that the naturalistic inquiry paradigm can be applied in several different ways (Lincoln & Guba, 1985, pp. 226-229). It can be used to conduct research (focus on a particular research problem), evaluation (focus on an evaluand), or policy analysis (focus on a policy option). Given that the inquiry methodology and criteria for trustworthiness apply to all types of studies conducted within the naturalistic paradigm, audit trail requirements and the procedures for conducting an audit of trustworthiness remain virtually the same regardless of the inquiry focus.

Regardless of whether he or she were concerned with a research problem, evaluand, or policy option, a naturalistic inquirer would maintain the six types of audit trail files displayed in Table 4.1 (Chapter 4). The forms of these files (i.e., paper files, hand-written entries, electronically recorded data summaries) would be similar. Changes are likely in the substance of information contained in the files. For example, the relative amounts of different types of records (i.e., interview data, observational data, and data from records or documents) may vary given a different focus for the inquiry.

Similarly, regardless of inquiry focus, both auditee and auditor would follow the same five-step audit procedure (see Table 5.1 in Chapter 5). Only minimal changes might be expected. For example, differences in the inquiry focus might necessitate rephrasing some of the language in the audit work program: An auditor of a research study might be more concerned with the evolving "theory" as opposed to an evolving "interpretation" of the evaluand. This difference is not simply semantic but reflects alterations in the context and purpose of the auditor's examination. Differences in the relative amounts and types of evidence available will require adjustments in the auditor's examination (for example, the auditor might be dealing with more records and documents in a policy analysis); however, these adjustments will not affect either the questions used to focus the audit or the overall intent of the audit examination.

Finally, regardless of inquiry focus, an auditor's qualifications must be matched to the type of inquiry in question. In Chapter 5, auditors of evaluation studies were advised to be familiar with the substantive issues involved in a given evaluation; the same holds true for auditors called upon to attest to the trustworthiness of research or policy analysis. Likewise, advice given earlier about methodological competence applies here as well. Regardless of focus, if a particular inquiry is largely an interview study, the auditor should be thoroughly familiar with techniques for gathering and analyzing interview data; if a study relies primarily on the collection and interpretation of documents and records, the auditor must be familiar with the methods of content analysis, historiography, and so forth. It should be apparent that prior experience in auditing will be valuable regardless of the inquiry focus.

AUDITING IN OTHER INQUIRY PARADIGMS

Our purpose here is not to debate the relative merits of different paradigms for conducting sociobehavioral inquiry, nor can we devote adequate space to describing differences in the assumptional frameworks of these paradigms. For present purposes, we will assume that there are two major social science inquiry paradigms, the naturalistic (also called the qualitative or interpretive paradigm) and the postpositivist (also called the quantitative or scientific paradigm). Each paradigm embraces a different logic of justification that includes (among other things) a different set of criteria for judging the trustworthiness or rigor of inquiry procedures and outcomes. (Readers interested in learning more about these contrasting views are encouraged to review Garrison, 1986; Lincoln & Guba, 1985; Morgan, 1983; Schwandt, 1984; Smith, 1983; Smith & Heshusius, 1986.)

The criteria of the naturalistic paradigm—dependability, confirmability, credibility, transferability—were defined at the beginning of Chapter 4. The criteria for judging the quality of inquiry designs and procedures in the postpositivist paradigm can be summarized as follows (Kidder, 1981, pp. 7-8):

(1) *Internal validity.* This is a criterion of truth value. It is concerned with demonstrating causal relationships by ruling out rival explanations, and spurious relationships.

(2) *Construct validity.* This is a criterion of both truth value and consistency. It is concerned with specifying correct definitions and measures for the concepts being studied.

(3) *External validity.* This is a criterion of applicability. It is concerned with establishing the limits (e.g., people, time, and setting) to which the findings of a study can be generalized.

(4) *Reliability.* This is a criterion of consistency. It is concerned with demonstrating that procedures for data collection and analysis will yield similar results if repeated.

(5) *Objectivity.* This is a criterion of neutrality. It is concerned with demonstrating that inquiry findings are not the result of inquirer predilections, biases, and so forth. Generally, this criterion is satisfied if the inquiry meets the first four criteria listed above.

These generally accepted criteria and techniques for achieving them have been defined in far greater detail by a number of methodologists (see, for example, Cook & Campbell, 1976, 1979; Cronbach, 1982;

Kerlinger, 1973; Krathwohl, 1985; Yin, 1984). Our intent here is to suggest changes in both the audit trail and the audit work program that would be necessary to audit an inquiry using these criteria. We think it reasonable to assume that, as was the case with naturalistic inquiry, only minor modifications would be required when auditing different types of studies (i.e., research, evaluation, policy analysis) within the post-positivist paradigm.

Audit Trail Adaptations

An audit trail constitutes a record of the inquirer's judgments that are not readily apparent to readers of an inquiry report. In a naturalistic inquiry, the inquirer is continually making decisions about data gathering, synthesis, and interpretation as the study unfolds. The product of the inquiry reflects these decisions, but it is highly unlikely that all of these judgments are fully discussed in the final product. To attest to the soundness or appropriateness of these judgments, the auditor examines the auditee's files, which contain a record of how, when, and why various decisions were made.

Judgment plays an equally important role in inquiries conducted within the postpositivist paradigm, as Cordray (1986) explains in the context of quasi-experimentation:

> In practice, quasi-experimental analysis falls somewhere between pure reliance on scientific methods and pure human judgment. A reasonable set of principles of evidence within quasi-experimentation must take this mixture of methodology and judgment into account. In particular, issues about evidence appear in two distinct tasks: the development of a data acquisition plan and the synthesis or combination of evidence into a coherent set of results. In both instances, the analyst exerts considerable discretion over the evidence to include, its completeness and relevance, and how it should be combined and presented in making a summary judgment about the strength of the causal relationship. (p. 10)

The audit trail of an inquiry conducted within a postpositivist paradigm should provide the auditor with a record of these kinds of judgments made by the inquirer.

From both the auditee's and the auditor's point of view, it would be advantageous to maintain the types of files listed in Table 4.1 (Chapter

4) and to provide an appropriate index and cross-referencing system. Within the files, one might expect to see data maintained in different forms. In addition to paper files and handwritten notes, there would almost certainly be much more quantitative data stored electronically. Depending on the forms of data maintained in the files, different types of indexes or guides to the files are likely. For example, raw data may be stored on a data tape. If this were the case, the raw data file would also contain a description of how the data were read on the tape. If raw data consisted of completed survey instruments accompanied by punched computer cards (reflecting a transposition of the data from the instruments to a machine readable form), the auditee would supply a codebook indicating how this translation was accomplished. If qualitative data were reduced to discrete units (e.g., phrases, sentences, paragraphs) for a quantitative content analysis, the auditee would provide a description of the manual or computer-assisted procedures used to accomplish this reduction.

Modifications in various types of audit trail files are likely in view of these different types of data. *Data reduction files* would likely contain fewer condensed notes of raw qualitative data and more descriptive computer analysis summaries showing basic descriptive statistics, measures of association among variables, correlation matrices, and so forth. The contents of *data reconstruction files* would reveal the link between theory, theoretical hypotheses, and empirical hypotheses; the results of statistical tests of hypotheses (either in a hypothesis-testing or exploratory data analysis mode); efforts to reanalyze data; various versions of data displays in tables or graphs, and drafts of final reports. Methodological and trustworthiness notes contained in the *files on process or inquiry methods* might include:

- discussions of measures (operational definitions) of concepts and the rationale for choosing certain measures over others;
- discussions of the means to establish the appropriate forms of reliability and validity of measures;
- descriptions of procedures used to rule out alternative explanations for hypothesized relationships;
- rationale for the choice of sampling strategy, including its advantages and weaknesses;
- (in the case of exploratory data analysis) notes about hypotheses tested and accepted/rejected;
- descriptions of survey administration procedures;

- rationale and procedures for assigning subjects to treatments;
- descriptions of treatments/interventions;
- rationale for selecting statistical tests; and
- formulas for complex calculations.

When appropriate, efforts to check the credibility of findings with relevant parties to an inquiry would be documented here as well. Audit trail notes might also include discussions of efforts to achieve triangulation through multiple definitional operationalism (Wimsatt, 1981) or critical multiplism (Houts, Cook, & Shaddish, 1986).

The file containing *notes about inquirer intentions and motivations* would be similar to that described in Chapter 4 except that far fewer personal notes would be expected. Personal notes are particularly critical in the naturalistic paradigm in which the inquirer functions as the major data gathering and processing instrument. Nevertheless, notes on methodological and theoretical preferences as well as notes documenting discussions with colleagues about research or measurement validity and reliability are equally valuable to the auditor of a postpositivist inquiry. Whereas notes about cognitive processes in the audit trail of a naturalistic inquiry would show an inquirer's decision rules for data reduction, these notes in the postpositivist paradigm would likely reveal the logical steps followed in deriving and testing hypotheses.

Finally, the requirements for files containing *instruments, tools, and resources* would be largely the same in either inquiry paradigm, though one would expect to find somewhat different materials in each case. Generally, the documentation of an inquiry or the construction of an audit trail in a postpositivist paradigm is somewhat easier. The procedures for these studies (if carefully followed) tend to leave a "natural" residue for the auditor's examination. Consider, for example, a survey research study: From the list of survey objectives (notes about intentions and motivations), the inquirer develops a set of questions for each objective (instruments, tools, and resources). The instrument is pilot tested and revised, and a record of the appropriate forms of reliability and validity is prepared (process notes). The sampling strategy and survey administration procedures are documented (process notes); raw data are received, coded, and descriptive statistics are prepared (data reduction files); analysis of the interrelationships— either hypothesized or explored—among variables leaves an output of computer analysis summaries (data reconstruction files), and so forth.

Adaptations of Audit Procedures

This section considers the adaptations that might be made to the five-phase audit model discussed in Chapter 5 (see Table 5.1) to accommodate an audit of trustworthiness in the postpositivist paradigm. The reader will recall that the five-phases included:

(1) preparing for the audit;
(2) assessing auditability and negotiating the contract;
(3) formalizing the contract;
(4) preparing and implementing a work program to determine trust-worthiness:

   (A) assess confirmability
   (B) assess dependability
   (C) review credibility;

(5) preparing the audit report.

Few adaptations would be required in the first three stages of the model. As described in Chapter 5, the auditee would initiate contact with an auditor; the auditor would meet with the auditee to learn about the inquiry, review the audit trail documentation, and make a pre-liminary assessment of auditability. Once an agreement to continue with the audit was reached, the auditor would inspect the audit trail more carefully, discuss the audit scope and objectives, and both parties would formalize an agreement to conduct the audit.

The requirements for a formal contract or letter of agreement would remain the same except that different audit standards or criteria would be specified. Whereas an auditor of a naturalistic inquiry describes the intent to audit against criteria of confirmability, dependability, and credibility, an auditor of a postpositivist inquiry might describe how the study would be audited against standards for construct validity, internal validity, external validity, and reliability. Obviously, that part of the contract containing the auditor's credentials would show the auditor's methodological expertise (e.g., quasi-experimentation, survey research, statistical skills) relevant to the inquiry in question.

The major change in the audit work program would occur in phase 4, the preparation and implementation of an audit work program. Here, the auditor designs a set of procedures to attest to the attainment of the criteria specified in the audit contract. We invite readers to develop a set of auditor tasks and associated focusing questions for assessing validity (construct, internal, and external) and reliability comparable to those presented in Chapter 5. For example, in examining the auditee's files, the auditor might judge the following aspects of the auditee's procedures:

- the selection of appropriate means to assess the validity and reliability of measures;
- the selection of appropriate statistical tests;
- the thoroughness of the search for rival hypotheses and attempts to rule them out;
- the extent to which data displays appearing in the final report correspond to earlier drafts of such displays;
- the appropriateness of comparing findings to the results of previous studies;
- the decision rules used to judge the credibility of various types of evidence; and
- the rationale for sample selection.

The auditor's tasks associated with Phase 5—preparing the audit report—would remain the same, and the structure of the report discussed in Chapter 3 would be equally relevant.

AUDITING FOR DIFFERENT OBJECTIVES

Thus far, we have argued that audits can be used to attest to the quality of inquiry given different foci for the inquiry (research, evaluation, policy analysis) and different inquiry paradigms. However, we have considered only one audit objective, namely, attesting to the rigor or trustworthiness of inquiry. Other objectives are possible. For example, the reader will recall that rigor (labeled *Accuracy*) shares equal billing with *Utility, Feasibility,* and *Propriety* in the Joint Committee's Standards for Educational Evaluations (1981). Thus one might argue that an audit of an evaluation should include attesting to all four sets of standards. (However, attesting to the trustworthiness or rigor of any given study may be the most important objective, for if a study is not judged to be trustworthy, it probably makes little sense to examine it against criteria for utility, feasibility, and so forth.)

We do not intend to debate the merits of different sets of audit objectives for different types of inquiries. Nor can we adequately describe all the possible combinations for what is essentially a two (inquiry paradigms—naturalistic, postpositivist) by three (inquiry focus—research, evaluation, policy analysis) by four (audit objectives—accuracy, utility, feasibility, propriety) analysis of variance. This final section of the chapter considers one different audit objective for one type of inquiry in the naturalistic paradigm: It discusses what an auditor and auditee might consider when the audit objective is to attest to the utility of naturalistic evaluation.

An audit conducted for the purpose of attesting to the utility of an evaluation involves determining whether the auditee followed generally accepted procedures in planning, designing, and reporting the evaluation so as to enhance the use of evaluation findings. In this illustration, the scope of the audit is limited to an investigation of the *evaluator's* procedures. In other words, the audit would not include an examination of whether and how evaluation results were actually used by decision makers or other stakeholders. An audit of evaluation *procedures* requires a set of standards for evaluator behaviors related to issues of enhancing evaluation use. An audit of evaluation *use* requires a set of standards for measuring use or user behavior.

A first priority would be agreement between auditor and auditee on what is meant by utility, evaluation use, or evaluation utilization. For example, the two parties might agree to an audit of utility in view of the Joint Committee's (1981, p. 19) definition of utility as procedures "to ensure that an evaluation will serve the practical information needs of a given audience." In this case, the auditor would prepare a work program to gather evidence of the procedures the auditee followed to meet the eight utility standards including, (1) identification of all relevant audiences to the evaluation, (2) demonstration of evaluator's competence, (3) selection of information responsive to audience needs and interests, (4) description of the procedures and rationale used to interpret findings, (5) preparation of a clear and comprehensive evaluation report, (6) dissemination of reports to appropriate audiences, (7) release of reports in a timely manner, and (8) consideration of follow-through in evaluation planning.

The work program for the audit would include focusing questions that would direct the auditor's attention to evaluator techniques relevant to each of the eight standards. Given the Joint Committee's definition of utility, it seems entirely possible to conduct an audit of utility with only minor modifications to the audit work program proposed earlier in Chapter 5. For example, evidence of audience identification (1), information scope and selection (3), and efforts to enhance evaluation impact (8) would normally be present in the auditee's process notes and reviewed by the auditor during the assessment of dependability. Information about evaluator credibility (2) and valuational interpretation (4) would probably appear in the audit trail file containing notes about evaluator intentions and motivations. An auditor examines this information in assessing both credibility and dependability. Evidence of report clarity (5), report dissemination (6), and report timeliness (7) will likely appear in both data reconstruction files and in notes about trustworthiness.

This illustration demonstrates several points: (1) it is possible to design an audit procedure for an objective other than attesting to trustworthiness, (2) standards for the audit objective (in this case, attesting to utility) must be specified, and (3) a naturalistic evaluation can be audited for utility using the audit work program specified in Chapter 5, given some modifications in focusing questions.

SUMMARY

This chapter explained applications for auditing beyond that of attesting to the trustworthiness of a naturalistic evaluation. It suggested that the audit trail and audit work program described in Chapters 4 and 5 are appropriate for auditing all types of inquiry in the naturalistic paradigm. Modifications in the audit trail and work program required to audit trustworthiness in a postpositivist paradigm were also explained. The chapter also suggested that the audit approach can accommodate a variety of audit objectives, and a brief discussion of auditing naturalistic evaluations for utility was provided as an illustration.

EXERCISES

1. Sketch the types of audit trail records that would be required to audit a quasi-experimental study.

2. Imagine that you have contracted to audit a study for aspects of utility as described in the Joint Committee's (1981) Standards for Educational Evaluations. What types of audit trail evidence would you expect the auditee to keep?

3. Refer to Table 5.1 in Chapter 5. In view of the discussion of auditing an evaluation for utility, how would you modify Event D in the table to accommodate an examination of the procedures used by an evaluator to enhance utility?

4. Imagine you received a call from a colleague saying that she wanted you to audit her study for "validity considerations." What questions will you ask her?

5. The Joint Committee (1981, p. 63) states that "Propriety Standards are intended to ensure that an evaluation will be conducted legally, ethically, and with due regard for the welfare of those involved in the evaluation, as well as those affected by its results." The Committee lists eight specific standards covering: (1) formal obligation between the parties to the evaluation, (2) conflict of interest, (3) full and frank disclosure, (4) public's right to know, (5) rights of human subjects, (6) respecting human dignity and worth, (7) balanced reporting, and (8) fiscal responsibility. Sketch the types of evidence that an auditee might maintain to demonstrate that he or she has met these standards.

REFERENCES

Accountants stray from their books. (1985, December). *The Economist,* pp. 88-89.

American Accounting Association. (1973). *Studies in accounting research No. 6. A statement of basic auditing concepts.* Sarasota, FL: Author.

American Institute of Certified Public Accountants. (1977). *Statement on auditing standards No. 17. Illegal acts by clients.* New York: Author.

American Institute of Certified Public Accountants. (1983). *Statement on auditing standards No. 47. Audit risk and materiality in conducting an audit.* New York: Author.

American Institute of Certified Public Accountants. (1986). *Statement on standards for attestation engagements.* New York: Author.

Ashbaugh, D. G., & McKean, R. S. (1976). Continuing medical education: The philosophy and use of audit. *Journal of the American Medical Association, 236,* 1485-1488.

Becker, H. S. (1970). *Sociological work: Method and substance.* Chicago: Aldine.

Bernstein, I. N., & Freeman, H. E. (1975). *Academic and entrepreneurial research.* New York: Russell Sage.

Besag, F. (1986, April). *Research ethics and why they don't work.* Paper presented at the annual meeting of the American Educational Research Association, San Francisco.

Bogdan, R. C., & Biklen, S. K. (1982). *Qualitative research for education: An introduction to theory and methods.* Boston: Allyn & Bacon.

Brown, R. E., Gallagher, T. P., & Williams, M. C. (1982). *Auditing performance in government.* New York: John Wiley.

Bulmer, H. (1979). Concepts in the analysis of qualitative data. *Sociological Review, 27,* 651-677.

Cahn, J. (1982). Legal and government implications of the ERS Standards for Program Evaluation. In P. Rossi (Ed.), *Standards for evaluation practice.* New Directions for Program Evaluation No. 15. San Francisco: Jossey-Bass.

Cassell, J., & Wax, M. L. (Eds.). (1980). Ethical problems of fieldwork (Special Issue). *Social Problems, 27*(3).

Chelimsky, E. (1983). The definition and measurement of evaluation quality as a management tool. In R. G. St. Pierre (Ed.), *Management and organization of program evaluation.* New Directions for Program Evaluation No. 18. San Francisco: Jossey-Bass.

Clemenhagen, C., Champagne, F., Contandriopoulos, A., & Pineault, R. (1985). *Hospital-based quality assurance.* Ottawa, Ontario: Canadian Hospital Association.

Comptroller General of the United States. (1981). *Standards for audit of governmental organizations, programs, activities and function* (rev. ed.). Washington, DC: U.S. General Accounting Office.

Conrad, P., & Reinharz, S. (Eds.) (1984). Computers and qualitative data (Special Issue). *Qualitative Sociology,7*(1/2).

Cook, T. D., & Campbell D. T. (1976). The design and conduct of quasi-experiments and true experiments in field settings. In M. D. Dunnette (Ed.), *Handbook of industrial and organizational psychology.* Chicago: Rand McNally.

Cook, T. D., & Campbell, D. T. (1979). *Quasi-experimentation: Design and analysis issues for field settings.* Chicago: Rand McNally.

Cook, T. D., & Gruder, C. L. (1978). Metaevaluation research. *Evaluation Quarterly, 2*(1), 5-51.

Cordray, D. S. (1982). An assessment of the utility of the ERS Standards. In P. Rossi (Ed.). *Standards for evaluation practice.* New Directions for Program Evaluation No. 15. San Francisco: Jossey-Bass.

Cordray, D. S. (1986). Quasi-experimental analysis: A mixture of methods and judgment. In W.M.K. Trochim (Ed.), *Advances in quasi-experimental design and analysis.* New Directions in Program Evaluation No. 31. San Francisco: Jossey-Bass.

Corsaro, W. A. (1981). Entering the child's world—Research strategies for field entry and data collection in a preschool setting. In J. L. Green & C. Wallet (Eds.), *Ethnography and language in educational settings.* Norwood, NJ: Ablex.

Covert, R. C., & Stahlman, J. I. (1984). *Evaluation '83: Reinventing the wheel—An evaluation of an evaluation conference.* Charlottesville, VA: Evaluation Research Center, School of Education, University of Virginia.

Cronbach, L. J. (1982). *Designing evaluations of educational and social programs.* San Francisco: Jossey-Bass.

Cronbach, L. J., & Associates. (1980). *Toward reform of program evaluation.* San Francisco: Jossey-Bass.

Dawson, J. A. (1980). Validity in qualitative inquiry. (Doctoral dissertation, University of Illinois, 1980). *Dissertation Abstracts International, 41,* 4686A.

Denzin, N. K. (1978). *The research act: A theoretical introduction to sociological methods* (2nd ed.). New York: McGraw-Hill.

Diener, E., & Crandall, R. (1978). *Ethics in social and behavioral research.* Chicago: University of Chicago Press.

Dunkin, M. J., & Biddle, B. J. (1974). *The study of teaching.* New York: Holt, Rinehart & Winston.

Edds, J. A. (1980). *Management auditing: Concepts and practices.* Dubuque,IA: Kendall Hunt.

ERS Standards Committee. (1982). Evaluation Research Society standards for program evaluation. In P. Rossi (Ed.), *Standards for evaluation practice.* New Directions for Program Evaluation No. 15. San Francisco: Jossey-Bass.

Fang, W. L. (1986, October). *Photography as a metaphor for qualitative methods.* Paper presented at the meeting of the American Evaluation Association, Kansas City, MO.

Financial Accounting Standards Board. (1980). *Statement of financial accounting concepts No. 2. Qualitative characteristics of accounting information.* Stamford, CT: Author.

Financial Accounting Standards Board. (1986). *Facts about FASB.* Stamford, CT: Author.

Flinders, D. J. (1986, April). *Being an ethical critic: A practical perspective.* Paper presented at the annual meeting of the American Educational Research Association, San Francisco.

Gaines, S. (1986, June 8). Accountants caught off guard by watchdog bill. *The Chicago Tribune,* pp. 1,6,7.

Garrison, J. W. (1986). Source principles of postpositivistic philosophy of science. *Educational Researcher, 15,* 12-18.

Geertz, C. (1973). *The interpretation of culture.* New York: Basic Books.

Glaser, B. G. (1978). *Theoretical sensitivity: Advances in the methodology of grounded theory.* Mill Valley, CA: Sociology Press.

Glaser, B. G., & Strauss, A. L. (1967). *The discovery of grounded theory: Strategies for qualitative research.* Chicago: Aldine.

Goetz, J. P., & LeCompte, M. D. (1981) Ethnographic research and the problem of data reduction. *Anthropology and Education Quarterly, XII*(1), 51-70.

Goetz, J. P., & LeCompte, M. D. (1984). *Ethnography and qualitative design in educational research.* New York: Academic Press.

Goode, W. J. (1957). Community within a community: The professions. *American Sociological Review, 22,* 194-200.

Gorden, R. L. (1975). *Interviewing: Strategy, technique and tactics.* Homewood, IL: Dorsey.

Guba, E. G. (1978). *Toward a methodology of naturalistic inquiry in educational evaluation.* (CSE Monograph Series in Evaluation No. 8). Los Angeles: Center for the Study of Evaluation, University of California, Los Angeles.

Guba, E. G. (1981). Criteria for assessing the trustworthiness of naturalistic inquiries. *Educational Communication and Technology, 29,* 75-91.

Guba, E. G., & Lincoln, Y. S. (1981). *Effective evaluation.* San Francisco: Jossey-Bass.

Halpern, E. S. (1983). Auditing naturalistic inquiries: The development and application of a model. (Doctoral dissertation, Indiana University, 1983). *Dissertation Abstracts International, 44*(4) 917A.

Holmes, A. W., & Burns, D. C. (1979). *Auditing: Standards and procedures* (9th ed.). Homewood, IL: Richard D. Irwin.

Holmes, A. W., & Overmyer, W. S. (1976). *Basic auditing* (5th ed.). Homewood, IL: Richard D. Irwin.

Houts, A. C., Cook, T. D., & Shaddish, W. R., Jr. (1986). The person-situation debate: A critical multiplist perspective. *Journal of Personality, 54,* 52-105.

Hudson, J., & McRoberts, H. A. (1984). Auditing evaluation activities. In L. Rutman (Ed.), *Evaluation research methods* (2nd ed.). Beverly Hills, CA: Sage.

Institute of Internal Auditors. (1978). *Standards for the professional practice of internal auditing.* Section 300: Scope of Work. Altamonte Springs, FL: Author.

Jacobs, C. M. (1973). *Procedure for retrospective medical care audit in hospitals.* Chicago: Joint Committee on Accreditation of Hospitals.

Johnson, K. P., & Jaenicke, H. R. (1980). *Evaluating internal controls.* New York: John Wiley .

Joint Committee on Standards for Educational Evaluation. (1981). *Standards for evaluations of educational programs, projects and materials.* New York: McGraw-Hill.

Kennedy, M. M. (1984). Assessing the validity of qualitative data. *Educational Evaluation and Policy Analysis, 6*(4), 367-377.

Kerlinger, F. N. (1973). *Foundations of behavioral research* (2nd ed.). New York: Holt, Rinehart & Winston.

Kidder, L. H. (1981). *Research methods in social relations* (2nd ed.). Chicago: Holt, Rinehart & Winston.

Krathwohl, D. R. (1985) *Social and behavioral science research.* San Francisco: Jossey-Bass.

Larson, M. S. (1977). *The rise of professionalism.* Berkeley: University of California Press.

LeCompte, M. D., & Goetz, J. P. (1982). Ethnographic data collection in evaluation research. *Educational Evaluation and Policy Analysis, 4,* 387-400.

Leitzman, D. F., Walter, S., Earle, R., & Myers, C. (1980). Contracting for instructional development. *Journal of Instructional Development, 3,* 23-29.

Levine, H. G. (1985). Principles of data storage and retrieval for use in qualitative evaluations. *Educational Evaluation and Policy Analysis, 7*(2), 169-186.

Lincoln, Y. S., & Guba, E. G. (1985). *Naturalistic inquiry.* Beverly Hills, CA: Sage.

Lincoln, Y. S., & Guba, E. G. (1986). But is it rigorous? Trustworthiness & authenticity in naturalistic evaluation. In D. D. Williams (Ed.), *Naturalistic evaluation.* New Directions for Program Evaluation No. 30. San Francisco: Jossey-Bass.

Lindesmith, A. R. (1947). *Opiate addiction.* Bloomington, IN: Principia.

Lofland, J. (1971). *Analyzing social settings: A guide to qualitative observation and analysis.* Belmont, CA: Wadsworth.

Madaus, G. F., Stufflebeam, D. L., & Scriven, M. (1983). Program evaluation: A historical overview. In G. F. Madaus, D. L. Stufflebeam, & M. Scriven (Eds.), *Evaluation models.* Boston: Kluwer-Nijhoff.

Mautz, R. K. (1964). *Fundamentals of auditing* (2nd ed.). New York: John Wiley.

Mautz, R. K., & Winjum, J. (1981). *Criteria for management control systems.* New York: Financial Executives Research Foundation.

McClintock, C. (1986). Toward a theory of formative program evaluation. In D. S. Cordray, & M. W. Lipsey (Eds.), *Evaluation studies review annual,* Vol. 11. Beverly Hills, CA: Sage.

McRoberts, H. A., & Soper, N. (1985, October) *Auditing program effectiveness measurement.* Presession presented at the joint meeting of the Canadian Evaluation Society, Evaluation Network, and Evaluation Research Society, Toronto, Ontario.

Mednick, R. (1986, February). The auditor's role in society. *Journal of Accountancy,* pp. 70-74.

Meigs, W. G., Whittington, O. R., & Meigs, R. F. (1982). *Principles of auditing* (7th ed.). Homewood, IL: Richard D. Irwin.

Miles, M. B., & Huberman, A. M. (1984). *Qualitative data analysis: A sourcebook of new methods.* Beverly Hills, CA: Sage.

Morgan, G. (Ed.) (1983). *Beyond method: Strategies for social research.* Beverly Hills: Sage.

Patton, M. Q. (1980). *Qualitative evaluation methods.* Beverly Hills, CA: Sage.

Previts, G. J. (1985). *The scope of CPA services.* New York: John Wiley .

Reichner, J. G. (1986, June 16). Auditor's role: Misperception or shift? *Philadelphia Business Journal,* p. 7.

Reinharz, S. (1979). *On becoming a social scientist.* San Francisco: Jossey-Bass.

Rothwell, W. J. (1984, June). How to conduct a real performance audit. *Training,* pp. 45-49.

Schandl, C. W. (1978). *Theory of auditing.* Houston, TX: Scholars.

Schatzman, L., & Strauss, A. (1973). *Field research: Strategies for a natural sociology.* Englewood Cliffs, NJ: Prentice-Hall.

Schwandt, T. A. (1984). An examination of alternative models for socio-behavioral research. (Doctoral dissertation, Indiana University, 1984). *Dissertation Abstracts International, 45*(9), 3007A.

Scriven, M. (1969). An introduction to meta-evaluation. *Educational Product Report, 2,* 36-38.

Scriven, M. (1974). Standards for the evaluation of educational programs and products. In G. D. Borich (Ed.), *Evaluating educational programs and products.* Englewood Cliffs, NJ: Educational Technology.

Sebeok, T. A., & Rosenthal, R. (Eds.) (1981). The Clever Hans phenomenon: Communication with horses, whales, apes, and people. *Annals of the New York Academy of Sciences* (Vol. 364). New York: New York Academy of Sciences.

Skrtic, T. M. (1985). Doing naturalistic research into educational organizations. In Y. S. Lincoln (Ed.), *Organizational theory and inquiry.* Beverly Hills, CA: Sage.

Skrtic, T. M., Guba, E. G., & Knowlton, H. E. (1985). *Interorganizational special education programming in rural areas; Technical report on the multisite naturalistic field study.* Washington, DC: National Institute of Education.

Smith, J. K. (1983). Quantitative versus qualitative: An attempt to clarify the issue. *Educational Researcher, 12,* 6-13.

Smith, J. K., & Heshusius, L. (1986). Closing down the conversation: The end of the quantitative-qualitative debate among educational inquirers. *Educational Researcher, 15,* 4-12.

Spradley, J. (1979). *The ethnographic interview.* New York: Holt Rinehart & Winston.

Strike, K. (1986, April). *Conflict of interest in evaluative research.* Paper presented at the annual meeting of the American Educational Research Association, San Francisco.

Stufflebeam, D. L. (1974). *Meta-evaluation.* The Evaluation Center, Occasional Paper Series (Paper No. 3). Kalamazoo: Western Michigan University Press.

Stufflebeam, D. L. (1978). Meta-evaluation: An overview. *Evaluation and the Health Professions, 1,* 17-43.

Stufflebeam, D. L. (1981). Metaevaluation: Concepts, standards, and uses. In R. A. Berk (Ed.), *Educational evaluation methodology: The state of the art.* Baltimore, MD: John Hopkins University Press.

Stufflebeam, D. L. (1982, October). *An examination of the overlap between ERS and Joint Committee standards.* Paper presented at the joint meeting of the Evaluation Network and the Evaluation Research Society, Baltimore.

Stufflebeam, D. L. (1986, April). *Standards of practice for evaluators.* Paper presented at the annual meeting of the American Educational Research Association, San Francisco.

Taylor, D. H., & Glezen, G. W. (1982). *Auditing: Integrated concepts and procedures* (2nd ed.). New York: John Wiley .

Thornton, S. J. (1986, April). *Ethical issues in the field: Taken by surprise.* Paper presented at the annual meeting of the American Educational Research Association, San Francisco.

Thurston, P. W., Ory, J. C., Mayberry, P. W., & Braskamp, L. A. (1984). Legal and professional standards in program evaluation. *Educational Evaluation and Policy Analysis, 6,* 15-26.

U. S. General Accounting Office. (1978). *Assessing social program impact evaluations: A checklist approach.* Washington, DC: Author.

Walter, S., & Earle, R. S. (1981-1982). Contracting for instructional development: A follow-up. *Journal of Instructional Development, 5,* 26-31.

Webb, E., Campbell, D., Schwartz, R., Sechrest, L. (1966). *Unobtrusive measures: Nonreactive research in the social sciences.* Chicago: Rand McNally.

Williams, D. D. (Ed.) (1986). *Naturalistic evaluation.* New Directions for Program Evaluation No. 30. San Francisco: Jossey-Bass.

Wimsatt, W. C. (1981). Robustness, reliability, and overdetermination. in M. B. Brewer, & B. E. Collins (Eds.), *Scientific inquiry and the social sciences.* San Francisco: Jossey-Bass.

Yin, R. K. (1984). *Case study research: Design and methods.* Beverly Hills, CA: Sage.

AUTHOR INDEX

SUBJECT INDEX

ABOUT THE AUTHORS

Thomas A. Schwandt is an Assistant Professor in the Center for Educational Development at the University of Illinois at Chicago. He holds a B.A. in English literature from Valparaiso University (1970) and an M.S. in vocational education (1981) and a Ph.D. in educational inquiry methodology (1984) from Indiana University. He has designed and conducted evaluations of secondary and postsecondary vocational education and training programs, management and technical training in business and industry, training organizations, residency and faculty development programs in medical education settings, and staff development programs in public schools.

His scholarly and teaching interests include the philosophy and methods of naturalistic-interpretive inquiry, the evaluation of educational programs, and the assessment of the quality of social scientific inquiry. He has published papers on both educational evaluation and the philosophy of educational inquiry.

Edward S. Halpern is a member of the Technical Staff in Systems Engineering at AT&T Bell Laboratories. He is responsible for designing and evaluating human interfaces of office automation features provided by large switching systems. Since he began working at Bell Labs in 1983, he has developed training courses, evaluated training, evaluated large-scale software development processes, and conducted product evaluations.

He holds a B.S. degree in economics (1974) and an M.S. (1978) and Ph.D. (1983) in instructional systems technology from Indiana University. While at Indiana, he began exploring the feasibility of auditing naturalistic inquiries for purposes of assessing rigor. This became the topic for his dissertation. He has presented several papers on applications of auditing to educational inquiry and teamed with coauthor Thomas Schwandt to design and conduct workshops on this topic.